IMAGINATION
A Future for Religious Life

Louis DeThomasis, FSC

For

Saint John Baptist de La Salle

and

his brothers

Fratres Scholarum Christianarum

243
Act 48

Religious Life

Published by The Metanoia Group, 700 Terrace Heights, Winona, Minnesota
55987-1399.

Printed in the United States of America

Printing: 6 5 4 3 2 1

Year: 1998 97 96 95 94 93 92

ISBN 0–9631835–1–6

Table of Contents

Acknowledgments

The seed of this work was the book *The Transformal Organization,* which resulted from collaboration with my co-authors Dr. William Ammentorp of the University of Minnesota, and Dean Mary Catherine Fox of the School of Business at Saint Mary's College of Minnesota. I am grateful to these two fine educators for their many insights and observations.

There are many more individuals who spent time reviewing the initial drafts of this manuscript. I express my appreciation to Paul K. Hennessy, CFC, Michael McKenery, FSC, and Sean Sammons, FMS. My gratitude goes to those at Saint Mary's College of Minnesota who helped me with their suggestions, especially Dr. Rosemary Broughton, Dr. Daniel Malone, and Dr. Justin Green, and also to the staff of Saint Mary's Press.

All of these people helped me enormously with their criticisms and comments. However, I alone am responsible for the use that I made of the many ideas I have culled from them, and from others.

LOUIS DETHOMASIS, FSC

Introduction

> If you think the Ten Commandments on two stone tablets are hard to
> follow, be thankful Moses didn't return from the mountain with a
> couple of floppy disks. (Reportedly told by an old prophet who wit-
> nessed an individual shouting this statement while standing next to
> the golden calf)

Speaking of computers now, a few thousand years after the old prophet
heard this proclamation about floppy disks, I overheard some computer
experts speaking in hushed tones about several of the nation's top computer companies. These companies pooled their resources and developed
the most powerful computer the world has ever known. They spoke of the
many specialists who labored during the past decade to complete this
computer, which stands as high as a five-story building. I then heard the
experts tell of the first day they activated this supercomputer and posed
the first question to be fed into this incredible machine: "Is there a God?"
In just 1.2 seconds the answer was printed. "There is now."

Should we be surprised or, for that matter, even question the veracity
of my supercomputer story—that today there are those who lay claim to
their creation of God. What an imagination it must take to create God! Indeed, it does take an imagination. Is that all it takes?

Now consider this story: It was said of the nineteenth-century French
short-story writer Guy de Maupassant that he ate his lunch each day at
the restaurant in the Eiffel Tower, because it was the only restaurant in
Paris where he could eat without looking at the tower. A 1990s marketing
strategy could aptly use this tale *de rigueur* to create a magnificent testa-
ment to the fine grand cuisine of the restaurant. It would be, of course, a
conscious twisting of the truth from the perspective of de Maupassant's
gourmand sensibilities and motivations.

Similar to Procrustes, who cut people to fit his ideas and not vice versa, such marketing license in today's culture hardly seems significantly
inappropriate, although it is a bit messy if the whole truth be known. Yet,
would such an imagination that manipulates the truth be any less trouble-
some at any other time in history? For instance, the imagination of Tycho
Brahe, a sixteenth-century Danish mathematician-philosopher, manufac-
tured a solution to Copernicus's then most distasteful revelation that the

earth was not the center of the universe. Brahe made Copernicus's discovery more palatable by agreeing that indeed all the planets revolved around the sun just as Copernicus had said; however, all those planets and the sun revolved around the earth. What a pleasant fabrication obfuscating the truth. Ah, but now, all would be well and tasteful—not a bit tacky!

Throughout history, patterns of imagination manifesting how men and women consciously dance around the truth defy even the most astute observers. We are all partners in a "dance" of standard assumptions, phrases, and actions. We live in a kind of procrustean bed that molds each of us to a form compatible with the *au courant,* no matter what serpentine road we follow around the extant reality. In an era when indignation has become a way of life:

- by conservatively disposed politicians making sure that everybody "pays their way"
- by the liberally disposed seeking a Robin Hood-type government
- by academicians seeking the "politically correct"
- by those supporting some miraculous intellectual *aggiornamento*
- by the media-hyped televangelistic purveyors of religion who have, of late, been an epiphany for all that they have preached against

Ideologues of all types abound! Truth is not an infrequent victim.

Men and women approaching the reality of the third millennium in a world that neglects vast and overwhelming human needs from problems such as poverty, oppression, and marginalization must have not only good advice to solve such horrors but excellent follow-through as well. We can no longer live around the truth that living standards continue to deteriorate for most of the world's 5.3 billion people, about 4 billion of whom live in Third World countries.

Effective action for the future demands nothing less than a global *metanoia* in the imagination of humankind—a change of mind, vision, and heart so radical that it makes the horrors of present reality unreal, while creating a future that could become real. Of course, it is difficult to sell us the reality that even in good times, we may have to do with less for the sake of others. Such a metanoia requires a courageous honesty among politicians, academicians, scientists, and churches; we must simply admit that our present ways are not working for the vast majority of people on planet earth. Save us from the ideologues who will, for certain, have their new faddish principles to herald as solutions. Let's stop being principled and do what's right!

We need nothing less than a paradigm shift, a new model of behavior. Our present stereotyped behavior has become inadequate in helping us face the overwhelming challenges of the third millennium. Thus, this behavior must be replaced. Granted this is easier said than done. To bring about this paradigm shift, we must first admit the futility of our present myths and metaphors, which reinforce technology's pre-eminence as mediatrix between problems and solutions. Mere mortals will find this feat difficult. These very shared values and points of view now help us compose an agenda of problems we judge worthy of our attention, identify the approaches most likely to arrive at solutions, and then act toward achieving these solutions. But our future cannot depend only on the use of technologies and machines. B.F. Skinner put it poignantly when he said, "The real problem is not whether machines think but whether men do" (1969, p. 288).

More than ever, if we are not to live around the truth, and if we are not to manufacture palatable lies like Tycho Brahe did during his times, we need the imaginations of not only the scientist but the poet, not only the technocrat but the philosopher, not only the computer programmer but the artist, not only the economist but the religious. Faith and finance, a new ruling paradigm, must emerge as a new and empowering force to bring hope to the unfortunate millions of men and women on earth whose lives are a reality of deprivation and desperation.

Unreality thrives when we permit the ideologue and the narrowly educated to gain power over our culture and dictate their myopic paradigms that, supposedly, will cure society's ills:

- End poverty. Just let the poor get jobs.
- Most of the homeless really want to live that way.
- Stop crime. Build more jails.
- Let the Third World countries first pay back their loans to us before we "help" them again.

Paradigms gain impressive power over what we think and do. They become institutionalized models that channel our daily work and our use of human and material resources.

Thus, when we speak of a "ruling paradigm," we are talking about the shared myths and metaphors within society that limit what we will do and how we will do it. Acceptance of a limiting and fallacious paradigm fosters a less ennobling spirit of humanity and creates the unreal by facilitating the manufacture of lies and consciously living around the truth.

Or, as the Italian saying goes, *se non e vero, e ben trovato:* if it's not true, it might as well be!

Consider then, how in religious communities we sometimes hear imaginative recollections of the "good old days": the days of thriving institutional endeavors, the great abundance of camaraderie needed to *live* the "Rule" (or was that suffer through?), and the large numbers of quality vocations. Unfortunately, nostalgia serves very little purpose other than continuing to allow our communities to relate our "war stories," which ultimately contribute to a deterioration of our present-day self-esteem. The tragedy is not the many fond memories that we have but the attempt to imagine that those memories must be recreated in today's religious life.

I believe there is a future for religious life, a vital, meaningful future. That future does not lie in the nostalgia of the past but in our imagination, which is alive today with power waiting to be unleashed. It is there, and it is awaiting an effective dynamic to make real its power to create our future.

In this book, I attempt to bring to bear the light of faith to the very structure and operation of a religious congregation, in a radically incarnational way. This is neither a theological, nor a spiritual, nor a doctrinal primer on the intricacies of relating canonical considerations to changing religious communities' mores or rules. It is far from that!

This book is concerned with the human dynamics that affect how religious communities must face reality and approach change in their cultural and organizational life. In essence, it involves pre-theological, pre-spiritual, and pre-doctrinal aspects of the most basic dynamics underpinning society and its institutions. This book is not a nice-sounding homily about the virtues of religious life. Rather, it is concerned with the very paradigms we bring to our most basic assumptions in dealing with our organizational lives in religious communities.

Paradigms. What are these most basic, pristine builders of our imagination? Essentially, paradigms are frameworks of thought, schemes for understanding and explaining aspects of reality, as described by Marilyn Ferguson in *The Aquarian Conspiracy* (1980, p. 26).

Though paradigms have become part of the latest jargon of futurists, they are not always understood by all as to their powerful effect on our most basic understandings of how we view reality. An excellent and thorough treatment of paradigms can be found in the book by Joel Arthur Barker entitled *Future Edge* (1992). In it, he defines a paradigm as "a set of rules and regulations (written or unwritten) that does two things: (1) it establishes or defines boundaries; and (2) it tells you how to behave inside the boundaries in order to be successful" (p. 32). In order to develop an imagination with an ability to anticipate and to innovate a future for religious life, an understanding and appreciation of the role of paradigms is essential.

We are all familiar with the cliché, "I'll believe it when I see it!" However, when you truly understand the role of paradigms you would more accurately conclude, "I'll see it when I believe it." In essence, "Subtle vision is preceded by an understanding of the rules. To see well, we need paradigms" (Barker, p. 153). Even to see who our God is!

For instance, look at a brief history of technology: the lever, the wheel, the printing press, the telescope, the steam engine, the radio, the airplane, television, the computer. Each has, in its own way and interconnected with other technologies, changed its contemporaneous world and, of course, the worlds to follow it. And it is more than simple metaphor to suggest that each technology was virtually deified in its own time: the inexorable compulsion of our species to turn means into ends, technology into technocracy, then into virtual theology. Although this is a phenomenon of all ages, the effect is magnified in the late twentieth century because of the incredible explosion of technology. Whenever we give something an inordinately high value relative to other phenomena, we make it a god. The computer, for example, is no longer our servant; it is our master, our mistress, our Wizard of Oz. We speak here of the tendency of the practitioners to deify their discipline, which is followed by the discipleship of the general populace to concur in the deification.

It is too easy, though, to place the sole burden for the multiplicity of gods in our civilization upon the scientific community. The principle is true in all human endeavor. Without taking sides on the issue, observe the combatants in the art versus obscenity controversy. Some deify the First Amendment; some deify Artistic Rights. Each side has tended to expand its moral force beyond logical constraints, and deified movements beyond their own importance. The encumbering blinders of moral conviction tend to limit our view of balance, decorum, and sensibility in life as well as in art.

We live in a world, perhaps especially in a country, driven by economics. Our gigantic, monetary house of cards is so delicately and precariously constructed by economic theory that even the builders have lost sight of the foundations. But the principle is—in spite of strong indications to the contrary—that some simplistic form or another of economics will hold things together, at least for today. The economists believe that with a passion. The public, which understands almost nothing at all about it, has become most willing to participate in the deification of economics as the cure for our national ills.

We are not a godless society. We are a society of myriad gods, each of our own making, operating under the illusion of the interdisciplinary.

Sometimes economists, artists, scientists, and others seem to hold hands in an interdisciplinary promotion of the common good. But here they seem to be confusing the truly interdisciplinary with the multidisciplinary and the pluralistic. Each is willing to admit the value of the other person's "god," as long as others are willing to admit the value of "my god." Camaraderie is confused with commingling. Pluralism becomes yet another god, perhaps more powerful than the rest. Lost is the real benefit of the interdisciplinary: the sparking of the imagination; the creation of new ideas whose sum is infinitely greater than all of the parts. We gallop into the future in separate chariots—not quite of fire—content with a dead heat at the stroke of the twenty-first century, equally first, equally last.

It is my firm conviction that with an abiding faith in our church and an imagination that will create a new reality, there is a future that will bring to religious communities a life more abundantly and life-filled with the mystery of Jesus' love.

I end this introduction with the words Joel Arthur Barker used to end his book:

> During the next decade many people will be coming around blind curves yelling things at you. They will be too busy to stop and explain, so it will be up to you to figure it out.
>
> If you have paradigm paralysis, you will be hearing nothing but threats.
>
> If you have paradigm pliancy, you will be hearing nothing but opportunity!
>
> I would submit in the context of all that I have said, that the choice of which you hear is entirely up to you. (Barker, p. 211)

References

Barker, J.A. (1992) *Future Edge.* New York: William Morrow.

Ferguson, M. (1980) *The Aquarian Conspiracy.* Los Angeles: J.P. Tarcher.

Skinner, B.F. (1969) *Contingencies of Reinforcement: A Theoretical Analysis.* New York: Appleton-Century-Crofts.

CHAPTER 1

Paradigms
for the Religious Life

Every religious has had the opportunity to live in a variety of local communities. For most of us, community experiences were shaped by the traditional paradigm of religious life. We shared an apostolate, gave form to our commitment through organizations such as hospitals and schools, and participated in prayers and rituals whereby we proclaimed our faith. All aspects of our lives reinforced one another, and we were secure in living out our vows within the paradigm.

As I look back on the communities I have lived in, one stands out as a vital representation of the traditional religious life. In that community, my fellow brothers were all teachers or administrators in a private secondary school where we attempted to educate the children of the upper classes in a Catholic tradition. When I look back on these years, I often recall the conversations and emotions associated with "the drink"—our early evening social hour. The good-natured hazing of one another and discussion of students seemed to me, at the time, to be the essence of community life: a sharing of experiences among men committed to an educational apostolate and to the students we served.

One person stands out clearly in these visions. He is Brother Marvin, a quiet, smiling man, then in his late fifties. Marvin was our self-styled "gofer," always ready and willing to take on the most menial task and discharge it with enthusiasm. Indeed, he became known for his rapid-fire stereotypic responses to the typical social question, "Brother Marvin, how's it goin'?" He would invariably respond, "Much better right now!" This would invoke the next steps in a well-known verbal dance where the questioner would ask, "Why's that?" To which Marvin would reply, "xxx reasons! One, Two, etc." where xxx was the number of people in the questioner's group and the count was accompanied by pointing to each person.

As this exchange suggests, Brother Marvin was *always* able to look at the positive side of things. At "the drink," the community took this to extremes by trying to coax Marvin into making a derogatory comment about another brother or a student. I can still hear brothers saying, "Hey, Marvin! What about Joey? In my class, he goes to sleep every afternoon.

What do you think about that?" After a moment of reflection, Marvin would say something like, "Ah yes, but Joey was up late last night entertaining the boys on his floor. He's very popular you know!"

After a time, Marvin's positive view of others became a serious challenge to the community. Brothers would cite the most extreme cases of deviancy in the hope that Marvin would concur in their judgment. All to no avail. Marvin would always find something positive to counteract their character assassinations.

One day, one of our English teachers came to "the drink" with a smug smile on his face. He was convinced that he had finally found a way to penetrate Marvin's view of good and evil. During a lull in the conversation, he said, "Marvin, what about the Devil? What do you think of him?" With only a moment's pause, Marvin retorted, "Well, I'm sure that he's very good at whatever he's supposed to do."

I offer the above vignette as an example of how the religious life can be shaped into patterns of behavior that defy even the most simple changes. It would no more be possible to change the hour of "the drink" than it would be to get Brother Marvin to give the Devil his due. We were all partners in a "dance" of standard phrases and actions that made up a kind of procrustean bed that molded each of us to a form compatible with community life.

The community gained this power over us because we had a common set of beliefs about our apostolate and shared experiences drawn from our years in novitiate and scholasticate. We had committed ourselves to a mythology that held that schooling made anything possible. Even the most severely disadvantaged student could be set on the road to success with our help. In fact, we constantly reinforced this myth with stories of those students who had "made it," especially when they had done so by overcoming personal and social obstacles.

The mythology of our apostolate went hand in hand with another myth at the core of our religious life. We believed that a rigorous application of the content and methods of Catholic education would not only save our students, it would guarantee salvation for each of us. Driven by these myths, we faced each new group of students with confidence and created community with symbolic support and superficial friendship. We asked no questions, secure in the patterns of thought and behavior that had stood the test of generations of religious.

What was hidden from us during these years was the fact that we were living a life that was not only unrealistic—it was *dead!* By insulating ourselves from the true nature of our students and the challenges they faced in modern society, we were perpetuating a form of religious life that was no longer functional. We too were *dead!* We were living out our years in unproductive irrelevancy, driven by a failed paradigm of the religious life.

This is not to say that we did our work poorly. Far from it! We educated our young people to levels that made them competitive in the careers they selected. We spoke to the needs of their parents and gave them comfort in knowing that their children were in the hands of committed religious. We also believed that we were responsive to the deepest concerns of others in our community and that all aspects of our lives were coming together in living testimony to the validity of our vows.

In effect, the paradigm of religious life was reinforcing a paradigm of religious education, and both were failing the test of modern society. The religious community was an island in a sea of change where none of the real issues troubling our members could be faced and resolved. Parents and students were living in an ancient model of the religious school and using it to search for a quality educational experience where religion was, for most, an incidental correlate of excellent teaching. The death of these paradigms was truly hidden from all of us by the ways we rationalized our daily activities.

Failed paradigms are everywhere in religious lives. Religious who have dedicated themselves to serving the sick have been overcome by the calculus of industrialized medicine; they can no longer minister to the spiritual needs of their clients without computing the costs of care. Those who reach out to the poor are submerged by the sheer numbers of persons in need; they cannot hope to find the means to meet even the basic survival requirements of an exploding underclass. Even the religious who work with parishioners find that traditional paradigms are poorly fit to a church that is ever more complex in its social composition and increasingly inadequate to the task of integrating the faithful into a working community of belief and action.

However, in the demise of these paradigms there is hope. It is the thesis of this book that the death of traditional paradigms offers an opportunity for a resurrection of the charism of Christ in new forms that can infuse the modern-day religious with the spiritual energy required in ministering to the needs of a new global society. If we use our considerable intellectual capital to analyze the reasons for the failures of traditional paradigms, and if we organize our new knowledge in the light of our past experiences, we can, I believe, find new paradigms that will enable us to transform our lives and works so that they might appeal to all those in need of the gift of faith.

Paradigms and the Religious Experience

The use of the term *paradigm* to describe religious life is expressive of a growing interest in the ways people pattern their lives and give structure to their organizations. When Thomas Kuhn brought paradigms to our attention in the 1960s, he was primarily interested in how shared values and points of view shaped the behavior of scholars and scientists (Kuhn, 1970). It was his contention that commonly held paradigms determined all aspects of intellectual life; they helped people select the problems worth working on and the approaches which would be taken to arrive at solutions. Rarely could a mainstream scientist transgress his or her paradigm; such behavior would be truly unthinkable and would put one at risk of professional ridicule (Costi, 1990).

Surely the same might be said of the forms and patterns of religious life. Shared views of vocation and mission determine which human problems are appropriate subject matter for religious involvement. In a more compelling way, the ruling paradigm defines the range of acceptable solutions. Let me offer an example of the power of one such paradigm.

In the school where Brother Marvin and I worked, our clientele was almost exclusively drawn from the suburban upper middle class. This existed in spite of the mission of our founder, who challenged the brothers with an apostolate to educate the children of the poor. The paradigm that gave direction to the life of our school had evolved to a point where we could argue that educating the children of the rich as to the condition and needs of the poor was an acceptable version of our founding vision. In effect, we were fulfilling our mission by passing on the responsibility of caring for the poor to our students. We did this for what we believed were sound reasons: we hadn't the means to deal with the overwhelming problems of poverty, and our students, especially the well-to-do, might use their money and future social power to take up our burden. Make no mistake, we did our work very well!

In this example, we can see the power of paradigm at work. Our shared vision of our mission allowed us to select a soluble problem—the educational needs of the children of the rich. The paradigm also gave legitimacy to the solution: passing the burden of the poor on to others who might arrive at a solution we could not (or would not) discern. Over the years, we shaped our original apostolate to one which fit the paradigm so closely that we rarely gave critical attention to our mission.

Paradigms gain such impressive power over what we think and do for several reasons. First, they are rooted in our deepest wants and fears, which we shape through *mythology*. Second, they are firmly rooted in our minds in the form of *metaphors* that capture the essential elements of life under the paradigm. Finally, paradigms become institutionalized as *models* that channel our daily work and our use of human and material resources. Thus, when we speak of a "ruling paradigm," we are talking about shared myths and metaphors that exist within an institutional model that limits what we will do and how we will do it.

For most religious, the role of myth is at the core of how we define our faith in action. These myths are generally drawn from the charisma of the person who founded the order and defined its apostolate. The founder's work is summarized in a saga or story that illustrates how obstacles facing the apostolic vision were overcome. When the founder has been canonized, the myth becomes institutionalized in the training of new religious and is used almost daily to give meaning to the activities of members of the order.

It is this daily use of myth that is most important to our understanding of the relationship between paradigms and religious life. When an individual religious faces the enormous challenge of the typical apostolate in the modern world, it is easy to become despondent. No religious can expect to see an immediate expression of the apostolate in their work. Instead, it is likely that each will experience failures of devastating proportions; failures that can only weaken commitment to the religious life. Myths help to soften the impact of apostolic reality. The saga of the work of the founder and stories of the victories of fellow religious provide psychic energy when we face up to the challenges of our work. When taken together, the mythology of our order is powerful support for the timeless nature of our mission and its capacity to speak to the needs of people across the generations.

Myth can also be found in the mundane discussions of daily life. Here it highlights the behaviors that "work" with our clients and fellow religious. Each of us can readily recall stories about the young people we have taught, parents we have counseled, and brothers or sisters who have lived in our community. As we reflect on these stories, we can clearly see that they are myths of religious living and apostolic work. The characters in the mundane myth are overdrawn to exemplify how conformity to belief and professional standards vitalizes what we do.

Myth alone cannot motivate action. It must be given a readily understandable form that can be shared by members of the congregation. Metaphor serves this purpose by capturing the essence of myth in a succinct summary that contains a core picture or image familiar to everyone.

As we share in these metaphors, we get a sense of "singing out of the same book." We know what to expect of our fellow religious in our daily work and are secure in the belief that our future will be, more or less, an extension of today's metaphor.

Metaphor is very much a part of life in an organized society. Our social institutions, our communities, and the organizations in which we work are extremely complex. If we were to attempt to understand them in detail, we would be paralyzed, unable to respond in the face of confusion. Metaphors enable us to cut through complexity to the core of essential understandings needed to integrate our work and thinking with those we associate with on a daily basis.

As Gareth Morgan would have it, ". . . the use of metaphor implies a *way of thinking* and a *way of seeing* that pervade how we understand our world generally. For example, research in a wide variety of fields has demonstrated that metaphor exerts a formative influence on science, on our language, and on how we think, as well as on how we express ourselves on a day-to-day basis" (1986, p. 13, italics in original). For religious, metaphor does all of these things and, in addition, gives form to the apostolate in a kind of three-sided relationship like that shown in Figure 1.1.

FIGURE 1.1

**THE APOSTOLIC FOUNDATIONS
OF RELIGIOUS PARADIGMS**

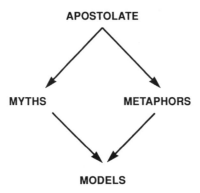

In any religious order, the *apostolate* is an abstract concept usually drawn from the personal experiences and charisma of a founder. If the apostolate is to become a guide to action in the present time, it must be given a durable form that can reduce its dependency on a particular historical context. This is the role of myth. The essential elements of the apostolic vision are embodied in simple sagas that carry the essential meaning of the vision to modern religious men and women. As religious represent the apostolate and its myths in their work and organizations, they come upon metaphors that express the essential meaning of religious behavior in a simple, understandable form (Pondy, 1983).

The religious community is one example of a metaphor experienced by nearly all religious. *Community* implies a group of like-minded men or women living and working together with shared goals. For many, the metaphor of community evokes a visual picture of religious life in a cloistered environment. In this vision, religious gain their livelihood and strength by directing their work and thoughts toward a common apostolate defined by a founder and interpreted by a director or superior. Thus, each religious is committed to the community and is sustained by it.

The community metaphor has also been extended to shape the associations of religious and their surrounding society. The Basque community of Mondragon in northern Spain is a case in point. It is a working example of how the social, economic, and spiritual dimensions of life can be integrated into a vital community. There, the community metaphor has woven the church into patterns of trade and social life so that each person has a meaningful involvement in both spiritual and economic activities (Whyte and Whyte, 1988). Those who live and work in Mondragon have a shared image of community that makes it easy for them to interact with one another and to draw on their collective contributions; they are the metaphor in action.

Myths and metaphors are the necessary foundations for behavior, but they do not define the particulars of our work. Nor do they determine how resources shall be acquired and used, or how decisions are made on a daily basis (Sackmann, 1989). These are the ingredients of organizational models, the explicit rules and practices that channel behavior for apostolic purpose.

In religious life, models take root in the *Rule,* the documents that translate the charism of the founder into specific guidelines for action. The prescriptions of the Rule are, from time to time, revised by communities to ensure that the charism of the founder can be implemented in useful ways in modern social systems. For it is only through such systems that the contemporary religious can have any effect on the social problems of our time. Models become reality in the schools, churches, hospitals or wherever religious live out their apostolic commitment.

It is in these working models that traditional paradigms of religious life are put to their most severe test. The social organizations in which religious live and work are shaped mainly by models drawn from the myths and metaphors of professional life, not from those of a religious nature. Thus, the religious following an apostolate to the sick in a modern hospital would confront a medical model that defined a view of the client and the healing professions quite at variance with apostolic vision (Ferguson, 1980). In a similar way, religious educators would be constrained by the ruling model of schooling institutionalized in their schools.

The effect of professional models on modern religious cannot be overemphasized. Individual religious at work in institutions shaped by these models are under heavy pressure to fit their behavior to professional molds. The result can be seen clearly in generations of religious who are often professional educators, social workers, or nurses first, and religious second.

As I see it, this last point captures the dilemma facing today's religious. They are confronted by powerful professional paradigms to which they must conform in order to utilize the expertise gained through training and experience. Over and against this, paradigms of the religious life are not particularly strong competitors. They are, for the most part, inarticulate expressions of the religious life *as it was;* they cannot serve as ruling paradigms in the modern world. Too many religious are attempting to balance the tension between a vital, working professional paradigm and a decaying, anachronistic failed paradigm.

The Failed Paradigm of Religious Life

As I look back on the experiences of life in our school community, I can see how we were attempting to order our lives by an outmoded paradigm. The myths and metaphors at the core of our thought were not translatable into a lexicon that could speak to the problems and challenges we found in our community and classrooms every day. The model of community life was also drawn from another time. We had replaced meaningful, useful rituals with superficial patterns of behavior that isolated us from authentic community experience. Our paradigm failed us, and we in time failed one another.

I now have a clear understanding of how we failed Brother Marvin. Our inability to penetrate his stereotypic behavior stood in the way of our understanding of Marvin the man. After I left our community, I found out that Marvin was a much more complicated person than the one I saw at "the drink." He was a combat veteran of World War II and one of the most decorated heroes of that conflict. The one or two who knew him in the 1940s told me that Marvin returned from the war determined to look for only good in everyone.

This remarkable decision pushed Marvin to ever greater rationalizations to explain the misery he saw in every newscast and the duplicity rampant among our students and colleagues. Marvin desperately needed to share his disappointments and to find new meaning from which he could renew his apostolic work. He needed a "paradigm shift," which would have made our community quite different.

It is revealing to consider that despite Marvin's evident need, the paradigm of our community life was so overpowering that even he could not ask for help. He could no more approach one of us with his innermost thoughts than could a poor child enter the gates of our school. Neither would be a "fit" to the paradigm. Each is an example of an anomaly that those of us living under the sway of the ruling paradigm failed to perceive.

It is my contention that there is more than enough evidence to conclude that the traditional paradigm of the religious life is a failed one. Even though it was "right" for many generations, the traditional paradigm cannot be bent to the circumstances of our times—it is dead! In accepting the death of tradition, we should not despair, for this is an opportunity for concerned religious men and women to develop a new paradigm that can enable us to discharge our apostolic vision in the context of modern business and human service organizations. The death of our old paradigm can lead to a resurrection of apostolic spirit and translation of frustration into creative energy, but only if we approach the task of paradigm redefinition with open minds and the confidence of a secure faith.

References

Costi, J. (1990) *Paradigms Lost.* New York: J. Wiley.

Ferguson, M. (1980) *The Aquarian Conspiracy.* San Francisco, CA: J. P. Tarcher.

Kuhn, T. (1970) *The Structure of Scientific Revolutions.* Chicago: University of Chicago Press.

Morgan, G. (1986) *Images of Organization.* Newbury Park, CA: Sage Publications.

Pondy, L. (1983) "The Role of Metaphor and Myths in Organization and the Facilitation of Change," in Pondy, et al., eds. *Organizational Symbolism*. Greenwich, CT: JAI Press.

Sackmann, S. (1989) "The Role of Metaphor in Organizational Transformation," *Human Relations,* 42, 463–485.

Whyte, W., and Whyte, K. (1988) *The Making of Mondragon*. Ithaca, NY: ILR Press.

CHAPTER 2

The Paradigm Is Dead! Long Live the Paradigm!

Since the time of Peter, the church has been at the center of forces that would change its form and mission. For the most part, the church has been successful in resisting these forces. It has continued to speak to the fundamental spiritual needs of its people through an institutional framework that channels the energy of believers in accord with its doctrines. In virtually every challenge, the church has emerged victorious, becoming stronger and more resistant to change.

The church has accomplished these goals by refining a basic paradigm, one that continues to draw on the charism of Christ to excite the imaginations of the faithful. The powerful myth of Peter as the rock on which the church is built is a timeless justification for the institutional metaphors that have evolved over the centuries. When the church speaks, we are hearing the voice of Peter interpreting the mystery of life in Christ.

Over the centuries, the founding myth has undergone a fundamental change. Many believe that when the church of today speaks, it is difficult to hear Peter—to say nothing of Christ. In essence, they believe that the metaphor has become the myth, and the chosen men and women of God have become the authoritative interpreters of an exploding body of controlling documents. The key word here is *control*. Some believe that all religious, no matter what their position, are controlled by the patterns of thought enunciated by the church. And the church, by extending and interpreting its doctrine, controls much of the daily life of its members. It defends the metaphor and lets the myth fade in the mist of history.

But the people taste of the metaphor and long for the myth. They want for the freedom of faith and personal empowerment that is in the promise of Christ. They long for the church described in the modern parable of Joshua.

Religion is beautiful only when it is free and flows from the heart. That is why you should guide and inspire but not legislate behavior. And to threaten God's displeasure when people do not follow your rules is being a moral bully and does no service to God. You

are shepherds and guides, but not the ultimate judges of human behavior. That belongs only to God. (Girzone, 1987, p. 253)

They do not want religious scholarship. They wish the charism of Christ.
But in their desire for a new church, they fail to realize that no solution is
possible without an abiding love and respect for the church and the magisterium.

Our longing for the founding myth is a force that has changed the paradigms of the church and the religious life many times in the past. Each
ruling paradigm embodies the responsibility of the church to the individual, to address the individual's needs and problems. When it fails, the
faithful call the ruling paradigm into question and begin to search for
ways to make the mythology of Christ work for them in the circumstances of the times.

This is a process of paradigm change that is cyclic and set in motion
by problem-solving failures of the ruling paradigm. In Figure 2.1 we can
see how these cycles follow one on another—set in motion by anomalies
or unsolved problems (Kuhn, 1970).

FIGURE 2.1

ANOMALIES AND PARADIGM SHIFTS

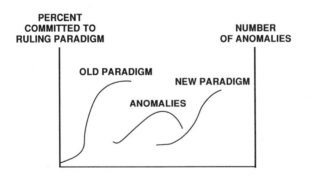

On the left-hand scale of Figure 2.1, we show the proportion of church
members who are committed to the current ruling paradigm. For any giv-
en paradigm, there is a gradual ascent to ruling status. When the monastic paradigm was introduced in the middle ages, it slowly gained
adherents until it reached its greatest influence in modern times.

On the right-hand scale, we see how effective the paradigm is as a
means of solving the problems facing the church. Using this scale, we can

evaluate the vitality of any paradigm by assessing the extent to which it enables religious men and women to address effectively the issues of their lives and apostolate. If a paradigm fails to evolve, it will begin to prove inadequate as a problem-solving tool. When this occurs, we see that anomalies increase, calling the ruling paradigm into question.

We can see how this works by considering a typical apostolate within the monastic paradigm: educational service to poor children. When this apostolate was carried out within secular communities of families committed to the paradigm of parish education, there were few anomalies. Virtually every child, rich or poor, was able to obtain a quality educational experience along with the spiritual values that made the child a productive citizen and church member.

However, as these parish communities became the victims of urban change, they became subject to major alterations in family and community structure. Poor people were no longer committed to the paradigm of parish-community, and they brought problems of increasing complexity to the doors of the parish school. When faced with these new problems, and with the lack of funds to remedy them, religious educators began to experience anomalies. Student problems could not be resolved, and the parish school began to fail some of its clientele. These experiences called the paradigm of schooling into question.

For many religious, the failing of the parish school as a community problem-solver occasioned the rise of a new paradigm. The paradigm was modified to one that cast the apostolate into a new form that essentially defined the anomalies of the poor out of existence. Instead of educating all comers in a parish school, some religious became professional developers of talent in what might be called "Catholic magnet schools," designed to attract only the most able and easily educated children. This new paradigm used the increasing professional expertise of religious educators to reach out to Catholic parents seeking a quality alternative to public education.

The Catholic magnet school paradigm rapidly gained adherents. It was (and is) extremely successful in honing the abilities of its students and in giving them a sense of the spiritual. These schools are doing exactly what the earlier parish schools did, only they are doing it for quite a different clientele. They are operating under a new ruling educational paradigm where few anomalies exist.

As this paradigm shift took place, it was easy to see how the thoughts and actions of religious changed to fit within the new paradigm. Most religious became, foremost, practitioners of their professions and, incidentally, persons who lived in community as traditionally defined. More and more religious sought advanced training in their specialty and, when programs of study were completed, areas of practice to best utilize their new knowledge and skill. Community truly became secondary: a place to live and, in ever-limited ways, a place to take part in spiritual experiences.

At the same time, apostolates were also reformed along professional lines. Master educators practiced their craft at ever more sophisticated levels. They would (quite naturally) seek out the most interesting professional problems where specialized knowledge could be used to seek elegant solutions. In some instances, the mundane problems of the many in need were exchanged for the fascinating problems of the motivated few.

Breaking the Paradigm

Following the above example, one could argue that the new professional paradigm hasn't really addressed the anomalies of the past. Instead, it has defined them out of existence. Given these changes, it's reasonable to ask whether the process of paradigm shifting could go in any other direction.

Of course it can. Many religious, and some religious communities, have faced up to the anomalies of the traditional paradigm. These people are what I would call "paradigm breakers," men and women who have a vision of a new paradigm that accepts anomalies and finds new myths, metaphors, and models to deal with them.

Sister Jean is, in my experience, the prototypic "paradigm breaker." She was one of the lead administrators in our school. In 1984, she drew our attention to the now famous report, *A Nation At Risk,* and challenged us to shape our apostolate to the reality of a generation of children in need. Unfortunately, her call went unheard by most of us. When we took the time to listen to Sister Jean, we found ways to rationalize our contributions to this national problem within the traditional educational paradigm of our school.

Fortunately, our lack of response did not deter Sister Jean from her vision of the educational apostolate. She entered a graduate program to study learners at risk and made herself an advocate for their cause at national conferences. She also took direct action to live out her apostolate by becoming the principal of a Catholic high school in one of highest risk areas of New York City.

Sister Jean's school was formerly a "white gloves" school for Catholic girls interested in careers in office practice. In recent years, the school clientele had changed from all white to a multi-racial mix of children at risk. Along with this change, Sister Jean found that staff members had lost confidence in their ability to educate their students, and the school was gradually losing its ability to train and graduate its students. In fact, the school was itself at risk of losing its accreditation and its ability to raise sufficient money to conduct operations.

Against these enormous odds, Sister Jean was amazingly successful. Her school now graduates ninety-five percent of its students, and all find employment in office positions where each young woman has a potential career. The staff of her school is enthused by its success and finds itself able to reach out across a wide cultural gulf to understand and meet the needs of learners at risk. In a recent review of the school by the Middle States Association, Sister Jean's efforts were singled out as an example of how educators could achieve excellence under the most difficult circumstances.

How did Sister Jean accomplish all these things? She did so by breaking the traditional paradigm of religious education. She centered her training on the needs of children, not on honing narrow professional skills. She challenged her staff to make extraordinary efforts to understand their changing clientele. She opposed her own religious community in order to keep her school open, going so far as to initiate a lawsuit that gave her the operating space to prove her case.

In the language of paradigms, Sister Jean observed the anomalies posed by at-risk students and recognized them as direct challenges to the educational apostolate. She also instituted a new paradigm for religious education by altering the conventional patterns of operation that had been in place within her order for generations. In these efforts, Sister Jean was driven by her faith, which was implemented through her professional competence. She drew upon the myth to create a new metaphor of schooling: the school as a one-stop human service agency.

The Paradigm Is Dead!

Alas, our religious orders are wanting for clones of Sister Jean. Too few paradigm breakers can share their visions of new apostolates and patterns of living. As a result, many of us are living in circumstances where the tensions of the times will create violent paradigm shifts, creating catastrophes waiting to happen in far too many religious communities.

I use the word *catastrophe* to suggest that not all paradigm shifts follow the smooth progressions laid out in Figure 2.1. The reason they don't is that paradigms are often under strains created by opposing forces, strains which can be in precarious balance so that ruling paradigms are at risk of catastrophic failure.

To see how this works, let's consider an example familiar to all religious—that of the Second Vatican Council and its redefinition of the religious life. During the 1960s, religious were becoming increasingly aware of lay apostolates in which men and women carried out meaningful work in spiritually nourishing environments. For many religious, the lay apostolate created questions about religious life that went to heart of the vows each had taken.

The Second Vatican Council also recognized the lay apostolate and attempted to accord those committed to it an appropriate status within the church. To quote from the *Documents:*

> In fact, modern conditions demand that their (laity) apostolate be thoroughly broadened and intensified. The constant expansion of population, scientific and technical progress, and the tightening of bonds between men have not only widened the field of the lay apostolate, *a field which is for the most part accessible only to them.* These developments have themselves raised new problems which cry out for the skillful concern and attention of the laity. (Abbott, 1966, p. 490, italics in original)

By taking this position, the council called into question all traditional apostolates and cut the ground from under many religious.

The effect of the Second Vatican Council on religious commitment can be pictured as the resultant of two forces: the appeal of the lay apostolate over and against the appeal of the religious life. The interaction among these three variables is pictured in Figure 2.2.

From the point of view of the Vatican Council II, the 1960s began with a relatively high level of religious commitment. This is represented in Figure 2.2 as point (A). By proposing a legitimate lay apostolate, the council immediately increased the attractiveness of this option to both lay and religious members of the church. Thus there was an immediate movement to point (B) on the "commitment surface," which shows the behavioral options open to religious as a result of the relative attractiveness of the apostolates. It was clearly the intention of the council to offer this option *only* to lay persons; religious were expected to remain within the bounds of the vows they had taken.

As time passed, religious leaders began to see a gradual erosion of their communities as religious opted to pursue their apostolates as lay persons. Figure 2.2 shows this erosion by the line labeled "Vatican II," which pictures such a gradual reduction in the "Percent of Religious Committed

FIGURE 2.2
VATICAN COUNCIL II: THE LAY APOSTOLATE

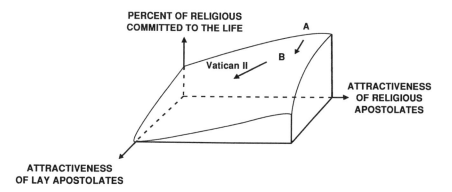

to the Life". Although church officials weren't particularly happy with this outcome, they resigned themselves to smaller religious congregations more strongly committed to traditional apostolates.

The events of the later 1960s called this sanguine view into question. There was to be no smooth, limited paradigm shift toward modest changes in the religious life. Clearly, the tension between the lay and religious apostolates was more fundamental than the council realized, and most orders experienced the catastrophic loss of commitment pictured in Figure 2.3.

In this drawing, we view the commitment surface from another angle. From this perspective, we can see that the surface is folded and that in the "Region of Paradigm Shift," it is possible for drastic—catastrophic—changes in commitment to take place.

This sort of folded behavior surface is representative of what social scientists call a "cusp catastrophe," which is due to the shape of the "Region of Paradigm Shifts." It is a way of picturing social situations in which two competing forces can cause abrupt, catastrophic, changes in belief or behavior (Woodcock and Davis, 1978).

In the case of the Vatican Council II, the evidence suggests that the paradigm shift was something like the path sketched from point (A) to point (B) in Figure 2.3. By offering the opportunity of the lay apostolate, the council set an adaptive process in motion along the "Commitment" surface from point (A). Movement of religious commitment to the left along this line resulted in putting the traditional paradigm of the religious life at risk of a catastrophic loss of support. This is shown by the vertical

FIGURE 2.3
CATASTROPHE!
THE PARADIGM SHIFT OF VATICAN COUNCIL II

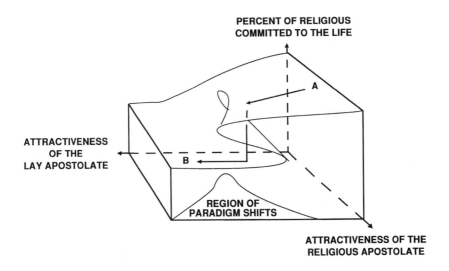

line through the fold in Figure 2.3 that results in a new, lower level of commitment to the life at point (B).

Vatican Council II was not, in the final analysis, a simple restructuring of the church and the religious life. It was the stimulus that initiated a paradigm shift of major proportions. When such major paradigm shifts occur, they are often triggered by relatively minor events or policies that tap underlying, competing forces. Endorsement of the lay apostolate erased a fundamental distinction between lay and religious and opened the door to catastrophic losses of membership in religious congregations.

Even the most casual examination of the condition of the religious life today gives testimony to the fact that we are on the lowest level of a commitment surface. We have lost great numbers of religious and have found it very difficult to recruit their replacements. If we are to rebuild the vitality of the religious life, we must think through the process of catastrophe recovery. Let me offer a few general principles of catastrophe theory as guidelines for a transformation of our life and work (Zeeman, 1977).

1. Paradigm Shifts: Forces underlie the commitment of people to any ruling paradigm. When these forces are in competition, it's possible for abrupt paradigm shifts to take place as we've seen under the stimulus of Vatican II. When such a shift takes place a new balance point between forces is reached, and the pull of alternative paradigms continues from a new equilibrium.

Religious life is still attractive to many in the church. However, its appeal is not nearly so strong as it was three decades ago. Now the lay apostolate has been shown to be a workable alternative with wide appeal to those who seek to serve others. The paradigm shift from the traditional religious life to the lay apostolate is a fact of life. The paradigm is dead! Long live the paradigm!

2. Irreversibility of Paradigm Shifts: When catastrophic changes of paradigm occur, they cannot be directly reversed. There is no way that the traditional religious life can be recovered by simple reaffirmation of vows or redefinition of apostolate. In the image of Figure 2.3, it's not possible to climb up the vertical line to the original plane of commitment.

What irreversibility implies is that the old paradigm must undergo fundamental changes if it is to attract committed followers. Its appeal must be forged along the lines laid out by the new paradigm, and it must compete directly and effectively if it is to become a viable candidate for the ruling paradigm. In other words, it is not the traditional religious life that we should seek to reaffirm but a new paradigm with many of the features that guaranteed the victory of the lay apostolate.

3. Inaccessible Levels of Attractiveness: Some of the balances between paradigm attractiveness cannot be achieved. Paradigms cannot coexist without one assuming a ruling status. Thus, Vatican Council II set the stage for victory of *either* the traditional paradigm *or* the ascendency of the lay apostolate. We can see this in Figure 2.3 in the "Region of Paradigm Shifts," in which layers in the "fold" are indicative of unstable commitments that must lead to abrupt shifts rather than compromise.

Inaccessibility is easy to understand when we think of it in terms of the relative problem-solving ability of paradigms. When the ruling paradigm begins to fail, it quickly builds up a reservoir of skepticism, and people are ready to take on any workable alternative. This was clearly the case in the 1960s when lay human service professionals were generally better equipped to serve needy people than were traditional religious. There was no compromise: one was either an ineffective religious or a successful lay professional.

4. Divergence of Commitment: There are points on the commitment surface of Figure 2.3 where small changes in relative attractiveness of competing paradigms can move behavior to either the upper or lower levels. The cusp of the "fold" in the "surface" is that point where divergence can take place. If the religious and lay lives of the 1960s had been at the point of the cusp, we might not have experienced the catastrophic loss of commitment. Instead, there could have been a more gradual change of commitment in favor of the lay apostolate. It is true that the traditional religious paradigm would have gone down to defeat, but in a more gradual manner and without catastrophic change.

5. Splitting Commitment: The tension between paradigms outlined above is what catastrophe theorists characterize as "normal" versus "splitting" forces. The ruling paradigm has a "normal" attractiveness due to its historical capacity to solve problems. People continue to believe in it because it has been successful in the past. When a new paradigm comes on the scene, its problem-solving ability is a "splitting" factor. The emerging paradigm "splits" commitment and draws adherents away from its ruling adversary.

Splitting is especially important for those dedicated to the religious life. Commitment is commitment, and it brooks no compromise. Religious men and women remain committed to the life so long as it enables them to follow apostolic vision. When it can no longer do so, they are "split" from tradition and eager to give their allegiance to an effective alternative.

Long Live the Paradigm!

Paradigm shifts are deeply troubling to institutions like the church. They call many of its tenets into question and draw the faithful into alternative organizations. In response, an effective church cannot rely only on its authority, nor can it trade only on its history. The emerging religious paradigm sketched out in the lay apostolate is a vital force that the church cannot hope to defeat by confrontation. It is a force that can, however, be shaped if religious men and women take heed of the arguments advanced in the above paragraphs. There are, as I see it, several concrete steps that we can take to energize the discovery of a new religious paradigm.

1. Abandon Ideology: We have seen that paradigms rise or fall on their capacity to solve problems. They cannot be held in place by ideology that clouds perception and makes the perceiver even more irrelevant (DeThomasis, 1989). Religious men and women must stand the test of their professional skill and the challenge of carrying the message of Christ within the arena of practice. If they cannot compete with their lay counterparts, no weight of dogma will draw the needy to their ministry. They will live out their years in the casket of a dead paradigm and will not hear the call to a rebirth of commitment.

Abandoning ideology is an especially difficult challenge for today's religious. They have chosen to live and work within the traditional paradigm, which has close links with Catholic ideology. As a result, religious thought and action is fully in tune with the pronouncements of the church and all members of the congregation are truly "singing out of the same book." What these people need is a "different drummer" who can show them the failings of ideology through the charism of Christ while maintaining that necessary abiding love and respect for the church and the magisterium.

2. Study Attractive Alternatives: In other words, know the competition. The personal and social problems of the needy will call ever more innovative paradigms into being. To the extent that they are successful problem-solvers, they will be competitors that merit our close attention. For it is through study and experimentation that religious can identify the new directions that will vitalize the religious life.

Religious congregations need more people like Sister Jean: people who can take objective perspectives on their apostolates and embrace new approaches to human need. These people are able to break traditional paradigms because they are truly *apostolic professionals* who use their considerable skill to reform mission to the circumstances of the times. Theirs is a life of continuing study and change in which the ruling paradigm is never settled. Rather, it is put to the test by the human condition and adapted so that it can carry the power of the myth to those who hunger for it.

3. Adapt the Ruling Paradigm: *Adaptation* is what breathes life into our paradigms. Once the ideological underbrush has been cut away and our paradigm is exposed to the light of social change, we set the stage for adaptation. But more importantly, we preserve a foundation for our work that enables each of us to draw on the institutional strength of the church and the magisterium to shape our lives and works in an adaptive mode.

As we have seen, paradigm shifts can be catastrophic. They can sap the energy of individuals and organizations and leave them adrift in a sea of change. In contrast, adaptation leaves the institutional framework intact and uses it to redirect resources and effort to new problems and approaches. This energizes the emerging paradigm and helps individual religious commit themselves to new missions and to approaches that meet the needs of today's society.

References

Abbott, W. (1966) *The Documents of Vatican II*. New York: America Press.

DeThomasis, L. (1988) *Monasteries on Wall Street? The Ten Commandments of Doing Business*. Winona, MN: Saint Mary's College Publications.

Girzone, J. (1987) *Joshua: A Parable for Today*. New York: Macmillan.

Kuhn, T. (1970) *The Structure of Scientific Revolutions*. Chicago, IL: University of Chicago Press.

Morgan, G. (1988) *Riding the Waves of Change*. San Francisco, CA: Jossey-Bass Publishers.

National Commission on Excellence in Education. (1983) *A Nation At Risk: The Imperative Educational Reform*. Washington, DC: Government Printing Office.

Woodcock, A., and Davis, M. (1978) *Catastrophe Theory*. New York: E.P. Dutton.

Zeeman, E. (1977) *Catastrophe Theory: Selected Papers*. Reading, MA: Addison-Wesley Publications.

CHAPTER 3

The Transformation of the Religious Life

The reason paradigms are so important for religious men and women is the close link between paradigms and organizations. Every religious community, each school, and the church itself is organized according to the tenets of the ruling paradigm. People are drawn to the religious life because their personal paradigms of the life are in tune with the structures and practices they see in church and community. Decisions are made according to the lines of authority laid down in the ruling paradigm's supporting documents. Even the apostolate is under the sway of the ruling paradigm in that it is defined by the organized activities carried out in its name. In a very real sense, the life is a tangible manifestation of the paradigm.

Religious men and women are bound to the ruling paradigm by the rules of their orders or congregations. In addition, they are drawn into their professional paradigm so that virtually all thought and behavior is circumscribed by a paradigm. Because these paradigms are the product of long periods of study and socialization, they are an integral part of each person's unconscious, controlling what one says and does. When these paradigms result in ideas and actions that work in daily life, religious gain confidence in their mission and the paradigm is further reinforced. This results in renewed commitment to the life and its organizations.

When the traditional paradigm of the church and the religious life comes under the kinds of pressures noted in Chapter 2, the anomalies of unsolved problems puts the paradigm at risk. It must change or lose all credibility. As we have pointed out, these changes can be gradual and adaptive, or they can be catastrophic. But one way or another, they must occur.

In the past, many changes in the paradigms of the church and the religious life have been brought about by scholarship. Men and women have studied the documents of the church and the Scriptures in order to ascertain how core values could be given appropriate organizational form. For the most part, these studies did not focus on how the paradigm fared as a basis for solving the problems of the church or the religious and their clients. It was, in a sense, up to individuals to make the paradigm "work" as best they could.

The contrasting approach that I am advocating emphasizes the social psychology of religious life rather than its documentary foundations. If we are to recruit able and energetic men and women to the religious life, we need to have a clear view of the capacity of our paradigms to liberate their problem-solving abilities. This, I argue, can be done only by knowing how the social relationships of the life affect the psychological dispositions of each member.

The psycho-social perspective I am advocating can be understood best by focusing on several key dimensions of the life. These dimensions are shown in Table 3.1 where comparisons are drawn between the traditional paradigm of religious life and a new *transformal* paradigm.

TABLE 3.1

ALTERNATIVE* PARADIGMS FOR
THE RELIGIOUS LIFE

ORGANIZATION	ALTERNATIVE PARADIGMS	
DIMENSION	TRADITIONAL	TRANSFORMAL
PURPOSE	Apostolate/Ministry	Transformation
CONTROL	Congregation	Stakeholders
MODE OF ORGANIZATION	Bureaucracy	Symbiotic
PERFORMANCE	Rituals	Social Justice
DIRECTION	Administration	Leadership
RESOURCES	Divine Providence	Human Potential
DYNAMIC	The Rule	Imagination
SOCIAL ECOLOGY FOUNDATION		

* The term *alternative* does not imply that the two paradigms are mutually exclusive, that the Transformal Paradigm should replace the Traditional Paradigm. Thus, Imagination does not replace the Rule as the organization's dynamic; Imagination is a new way of transforming the Rule so that it becomes an effective dynamic for religious communities.

The dimensions offered in Table 3.1 are put in place to give some concrete shape to our discussion of paradigms. Each dimension refers to an aspect of religious life that has a direct effect on how religious think about what they do; how they interact with one another and their clients; how they organize and direct their activities toward the goals of their communities. They are familiar to all of us as we reflect on our experiences as religious. In the Traditional Paradigm, we find much that is familiar. These are the aspects of the life that have both sustained and frustrated us. They are the critical defining features of the paradigm that put it at risk in the turbulent environment of contemporary times.

With this thought in mind, I have tried to select words that will draw clear distinctions between the alternative paradigms. To do this, I have made use of the two metaphors; that of the "Traditional Community" versus the "Transformal Ecology." In using the metaphor of ecology, I am thinking of the religious as a small frog in a complex, world-sized pond. We can no longer be isolated in self-sufficient communities. Instead, we must take the plunge into a world society in which our destiny is shaped by waves of change that originate from dimly seen shores. Thus, the whole issue of paradigm change is based on the Transformal Ecology, and all dimensions of Table 3.1 rest on this ecological foundation.

Metaphors such as *community* and their associated words and thoughts are the stuff of organizational life. As one writer puts it, ". . . all our ideas and behavior [are] reflections of some metaphor." Moreover, metaphors "[are] enacted and reflected in our actions and passions, as in our patterns of thought and behavior" (Wheeler, 1987, p. 224). Thus the words collected under the Traditional Paradigm above are expressive of the ways religious have come to view their world. They facilitate work and life within the community model, and they prevent us from seeing the threats and opportunities facing us in the future.

As you read down the column of words describing the new ecology of religious life, you will get a sense of the way each dimension of the life is affected by forces outside church and the order. Take, for instance, the dimension of *control*. In the past, control was vested in the congregation. Religious men and women ordered their affairs according to the Rule and sometimes paid little attention to the opinions of people outside the community. In contrast, the ecology of contemporary religious life is one that is controlled by stakeholders who have an interest in the purpose of the order. This makes the life of each religious interdependent with that of his or her clients and brings all activity under the sway of global social and economic forces.

In the paragraphs below, I attempt to draw the distinctions between the Traditional and the Transformal Paradigms more clearly. If you will follow along with my argument, you may begin to see how the ecological metaphor can help all of us make better use of our professional potential within the framework of our commitment to the mythology of Christ and the teachings of the magisterium about the Savior of our world.

PURPOSE:

DIMENSION	TRADITIONAL	TRANSFORMAL
PURPOSE	Apostolate/Ministry	Transformation

No organized human activity can exist without purpose. We come together in our churches, schools, and communities to achieve shared purpose. In fact, it is the power of organizations to focus resources on purpose that constitutes the defining characteristic of modern society. Without purpose, we are truly nothing; we have no rationale for what we do and no motivation to create the mechanisms that enable us to "do." Thus, when purpose changes, organizations must adapt or go out of existence. This is abundantly clear as we examine the contrast in purpose of the competing paradigms of the religious life.

Traditional Apostolate/Ministry: In the traditional life, purpose is manifest as the personal commitment of each individual religious to the apostolate or ministry defined by the order to which one belongs. Traditional purpose specifies quite precisely the services religious are to perform and the beneficiaries of their work. There is little latitude for the religious (or the client) to identify new needs and no option to shape the apostolate so that it can truly minister to human needs.

A familiar example of the traditional purpose at work is the elementary or secondary school operated by a religious order. These schools give concrete form to purpose through the curriculum offered where secular and spiritual issues are balanced according to the views of religious superiors. The visibility of the apostolate in these schools draws clients who hold similar views, with the result that the apostolate is reinforced and nurtured by the joint commitment of religious and clients.

When tradition breaks down, clients no longer conform to familiar patters of thought and behavior. The religious school that suddenly receives large numbers of at-risk learners is a case in point. These are students who need basic behavioral, social and survival training before they can adapt to the expectations of the traditional school (Faller, 1990). Because the school is constrained by its definition of purpose, it cannot adapt and, at times, those children who are most in need are turned away.

Transformation: The Transformal Paradigm effectively turns the above relationship on its head. By *transformation,* I mean to imply that it is the client who defines the relationship between those who are served and the religious who would provide needed services. From this new view of purpose comes a new organization, one that is mutually determined by the interactions between religious and those they serve. Unlike old apostolates and ministries that accept only a defined role in society, transformation seeks new opportunities to be of service. Consequently, religious living in the Transformal Paradigm continually refine their professional contributions to extend the charism of Christ to those most in need. At the same time, they seek out pressure points where their efforts might transform organizations or larger social-political systems.

CONTROL:

DIMENSION	TRADITIONAL	TRANSFORMAL
CONTROL	Congregation	Stakeholders

Organized pursuit of purpose implies control. Organizations must be able to issue authoritative commands and directions that will be followed by both members and clients. It is the source of authority that gives leaders the capacity to control the organization; their actions are effectively legitimized by the foundations on which control rests. At the same time, control gives form to purpose.

The actions that result from control determine the extent to which purpose will be realized. Over time, successful attainment of purpose reinforces control and vice versa. This means that the effective organization gains control over its members and enhances its capacity to enlarge purpose.

Traditional Congregation: Religious organizations have traditionally controlled the activities of members through their congregations. During our formation, we became aware of the link between our collective work and commitment and the charism of our founder. In the history of each religious order, certain events, when taken together, make up the "memory" of the organization and provide a powerful rationalization for the patterns of our lives. When we took our vows, we were essentially buying into this congregational memory and accepting its rituals and controls as molds for our lives and work.

The same can be said for the beneficiaries of our work. Those whom we serve have also bought into the congregation, and their behavior is controlled by its patterns and rules as they form relationships with us. But it is in these relationships that the Traditional Paradigm loses its capacity to control. Our clients are no longer drawn from a single ethnic group, one parish, or even from one set of beliefs. Instead, they come to us in need from all segments of an ethnically-diverse society, bringing with them cultural perspectives and experiences unfamiliar to us. When their demands and needs are filtered through the control of the congregation, there is no room for the flexibility and innovation called for by their condition.

Transformal Stakeholders: In the Transformal Paradigm, control penetrates the organization from the outside. Religious are no longer insulated from their constituencies by the congregation. Instead, those who have a stake in the purpose of the order are drawn into a relationship that gives them a substantial degree of control over the activities of religious men and women. This makes possible a mutual adaptation between the client's condition and the Transformal Purpose that has drawn that person to us.

The key word in understanding how stakeholders exercise control in the Transformal Paradigm is *mutuality*. Religious working under this new paradigm haven't given up control over what they do. They have effectively shared control with all others who have a stake in the work of the order. In practical terms, the professional life of the transformed religious is one in which the form and scope of purpose is in flux and is jointly determined by the interaction between religious and all stakeholders.

MODE OF ORGANIZATION:

DIMENSION		TRADITIONAL	TRANSFORMAL
MODE OF ORGANIZATION		Bureaucracy	Symbiotic

As organizations mature, control practices become institutionalized in roles and procedures so that everyone involved senses control and responds to it. These institutional forms become part of the metaphors and models that drive organizations and characterize them to those outside their boundaries (Morgan, 1986). In speaking of *pattern* in the above paragraphs, I was referring to the mode of organization whereby the daily activities of religious are ordered and directed. This pattern is what we have in mind when we choose a metaphor to describe the life. Thus, when religious characterize their lives as "family" experiences, they are calling on our memory of a paternalistic or maternalistic mode of organization whereby an older authority takes our needs into account and protects us from the mistakes we might make, were we to determine our actions ourselves.

Traditional Bureaucracy: Even though many of us would like to use the family metaphor to describe our communities, the unhappy reality is that we are really a part of a worldwide bureaucracy. We are very much under the sway of our written rules. Indeed, considerable time and effort go toward congresses and chapters in which the fine points of rules are debated and minute changes made. It is my contention that any close examination of the work of these groups will show that nothing has really changed in the mode of organization. If anything, the bureaucracy has been strengthened by our efforts, and we have constructed procrustean beds of rules and regulations that stifle the imagination and creativity of religious.

There is, of course, a reason why we are accepting of the bureaucratic environment in which we live: it guarantees our place in the organized pursuit of the apostolate and removes any pressure we might feel to find alternative ministries or to serve different stakeholders. Bureaucracy breeds complacency and a false sense of security. That is its principle weakness in a time when the only person who knows what needs to be done or how to do it is the religious who is directly involved with clients.

Transformal Symbiosis: I have taken the ecological term symbiotic to describe how religious groups need to organize for the future. This choice is made to indicate that we are interdependent with our clients and the social and economic environment. We cannot exist without intercourse with them, nor can we continue our work without their support. At the same time, they have pressing needs for the social services and spiritual direction that only religious can provide. We are in symbiotic relationship with them.

In the biologic community, symbiosis not only connotes interdependence, it also implies an exchange of energy that is beneficial to all parties in the relationship. The same is true for the transformal religious organization. Religious groups can acquire energy by engaging stakeholders in transformation of society—to change the life chances of the personal life and to transform the social order. The transformal religious organization can also energize those individuals and groups around it to make their activities more effective and mutually beneficial. In this way, a true symbiotic relationship is forged, one that is adaptive and, at the same time, resistant to destructive forces.

PERFORMANCE:

DIMENSION		TRADITIONAL	TRANSFORMAL
PERFORMANCE		Rituals	Social Justice

In the final analysis, the purpose of any organization must be measured so that its use of resources can be weighed against what it has accomplished. The measures of performance must also reflect how individuals and groups within the organization have contributed to the attainment of common purpose. In a very real sense, organizations unable to agree upon objective performance indicators are doomed to drift on a sea of confusion where the tempests of social and economic change can put them at risk of wreck.

Traditional Rituals: When I selected *rituals* as the measure of performance for traditional religious, I was struck by the unkindness of the word. At first reading, it seemed to me to speak of mindless conformity that was effectively without purpose. Surely this wasn't the way I saw my own life as a religious. But why was I drawn to the word? The answer lies, I believe, in the patterns that I associate with ritual. These can range from the rites and ceremonies symbolic of religious life to the pattern of our interactions with our clients and the outside world. In this sense, performance in the Traditional Paradigm is measured by the extent to which religious engage in the ritualistic behavior mandated by the congregation and the larger church.

If one accepts this view of ritualistic performance, it is easy to see why it is not a particularly effective way to assess the working of the modern religious organization. The very nature of ritual ensures that the organization will be unable to adapt to changing circumstances. Our schools will be irrelevant for at-risk learners; our hospitals will fail to engage patients on a human scale; and our nursing homes will be custodial rather than communal. By holding on to rituals in the environment of these organizations, religious are virtually guaranteeing their own demise.

Transformal Social Justice: In the Transformal Paradigm, we are taking a much wider view of performance. It is not measured in the narrow professional views of educators, nurses and administrators. Quite the contrary! The gauge of performance is the extent to which religious organizations contribute to social justice. Thus, the activities of every religious are evaluated as to the extent to which they help meet ". . . the specific needs of human beings—man or woman, child or old person . . . [and] a lively awareness of the value and rights of all and of each person" (Pope John Paul II, 1988, p. 13).

But isn't this what we always have been about? I think not. Many orders have strayed from their original apostolates and ministries to serve in convenient ways. It is, for example, far more common to find Catholic schools educating the elite than to discover them serving the poor. When our work is viewed under the light of social justice, it often fails on the ground that it does not benefit all persons. Today, the paradigm shift called for requires us to recognize the fact that each of us is in a symbiotic relationship with the poorest Third World child as well as with the most affluent suburbanite. This is the measure of social justice by which we are to be evaluated.

DIRECTION:

DIMENSION		TRADITIONAL	TRANSFORMAL
DIRECTION		Administration	Leadership

If an organization of any size is to fulfill its purpose, it must devise means for making decisions and coordinating the many activities of its members. This is the familiar role of management, one that is familiar to all of us. When we think of managers in instances of paradigm shifts, we are tempted to assign them their traditional tasks, and we are, consequently, led to expect that the work of the organization will proceed as usual.

It is this acquiescence to management that has stood in the way of countless paradigm changes in the past. By failing to consider new approaches to direction, those who advocate a paradigm change will inevitably come up against decisions and policies designed to preserve older models of organizational life. Consider, for instance, the following distinction between traditional and transformal provisions for direction.

Traditional Administration: In the bureaucratized environment of the Traditional Paradigm, direction is a matter of administration. Each order has its hierarchy of officials who interpret rules and assign priorities to apostolic activities. These men and women are a powerful conservative force in that they have the capacity (and the authority) to reject new ventures and, as a result, to stand firm in the face of paradigm change. Many of us have had the experience of proposing a new apostolate, or different pattern for the life, only to be frustrated by an administrative directive. When we have gone away in despair or, in extreme cases, left the religious life, we have given way to a direction destructive of potentially vital ministries.

The power of administration is enhanced within religious communities by the necessary and *de facto* hierarchical nature of the church. Historically, centralism in the church has been accepted *de fide,* as the way it must be in religious orders. As a result, it has created a mentality in most religious that is accepting of administrative decrees and reluctant to raise issues for debate or action. These men and women have become, in effect, docile and passive (or even passive aggressive) individuals who give reflexive responses to those in power. And so long as administrators and religious stride in lock step, there can be no hope of productive paradigm change.

Transformal Leadership: The fundamental contrast between direction in the two paradigms has to do with the ways people are chosen for management roles. In the Traditional Paradigm, seniority and conformity to purpose and control are the selection factors that give religious access to power. There is diminished provision for consideration of the opinions of rank and file religious. The Transformal Paradigm, on the other hand, emphasizes the concerns of stakeholders in selecting leaders. These are people who have a visionary picture of the working of their purpose and a capacity to excite clients, religious ,and vocations toward achieving its goals.

This shift of emphasis in direction means that a very different sort of person is needed in the transformed community. The man or woman who would direct an order must be, first of all, a person who has the capacity to imagine new ministries and ways to pursue them. But this individual must also be a highly skilled manager who knows the ins and outs of modern organizational activity. At the center of an effective leadership style will be the ability to see how resources can be acquired and orchestrated to enable the transformed apostolate to sing out to those in need (DeThomasis, 1987).

RESOURCES:

DIMENSION	TRADITIONAL	TRANSFORMAL
RESOURCES	Divine Providence	Human Potential

Nearly every definition of organization includes some reference to the acquisition and use of resources. Purpose is not achieved by decree or wish. It is realized only by the application of people, commitment and money to specific tasks. Organizations differ considerably in how they use these resources, so much so that we can draw clear distinctions among them as to their primary resources.

Traditional Divine Providence: God will provide! How many times have these three words been used by religious organizations to appeal for resources? How many parish schools have failed when the appeal has gone unanswered? How often has each of us turned to God when faced with budgets that cannot be balanced? The answer is, countless times!

Our confidence in Divine Providence was, perhaps, justified. Religious organizations were a part of a seamless web with the church at its center. When any link in the web became at risk, other entities rushed to its rescue, and it was quite correct to assume that the hand of God was at work to provide the resources needed.

Transformal Human Potential: As the web of religious organizations has unraveled in recent decades, it has seemed as if God has forsaken us. But let's be realistic! There probably will be no literal repetitions of the miracle of the loaves and fishes! The miracle is within each of us. We have the human potential to energize our work at the practical level. Let God provide our spiritual strength so that we can get about the business of acquiring and using resources in pursuit of His purpose.

DYNAMIC:

DIMENSION	TRADITIONAL	TRANSFORMAL
DYNAMIC	The Rule	Imagination

There is, as I see it, a mystic force that energizes the members of any successful organization. This force is not the same spiritual energy we associate with the religious life—although it is much like it. In most organizations, the dynamic derives from a founding person or concept and retains its vitality to the extent that the organization achieves its goals. Dynamic is what makes business organizations such as IBM able to weather financial storms, to grow in wealth and power, and to capture the loyalty of employees. Dynamic is what made the Jesuits invincible soldiers of Christ, able to carry his message to the needy in the face of incredible obstacles.

Dynamic is not, alas, itself invincible. Like people and organizations, dynamism can be weakened by changing circumstances and organizational failure. We all know about organizations such as U.S. Steel, where international competition effectively destroyed a powerful labor dynamic. We also have experienced erosion of our own dynamics—although we have trouble admitting to their failure. In my judgment, this is the most serious impediment to the transformation I am calling for in this book.

Traditional Rule: At this point in your reading, you should be getting the impression that I see the traditional religious life as highly controlled with little potential for productive change. I hold this belief because I see us following a dynamic that is too closely bound to the past. Like many of you, I have participated in countless deliberations about the future—but they have invariably been shaped by the Rule and its interpretation of the charism of our founder. Too often these debates have concluded with minor changes to the Rule. When taken back to our daily work, they fail to renew our energy and commitment because these discussions have relied on old myths and metaphors no longer potent in today's world.

The historical continuity expressed in our Rule can be a source of both strength and weakness. The considerable success we have achieved in the past can be ascribed to the balance between the Rule and the social and economic circumstances in which we work. These successes strengthen us and make it difficult to call the Rule into question. However, when circumstances undergo the cataclysmic changes now under way, the Rule prevents adaptation. It is, then, a failed dynamic that must be replaced, else we lose relevance and become dying vestiges of the past.

Transformal Imagination: The paradigm shift here is one from documents to mind. In place of written rules, there is a dynamic of imagination that unleashes the creative abilities of all religious. It is imagination that forges the link tying all stakeholders into one body, sharing in the charism of Christ and the founders of our orders to feed our spiritual needs. This same Imagination has its practical side that visualizes the relationship between the religious life and its surroundings; it is a unique blend of the spiritual and the mundane.

Although I have presented a gloomy view of the traditional life, I continue to have confidence in my fellow religious. We have the capacity to create a new life by imagining new ministries and the organizational forms to pursue them. If we have the courage to set imagination free, I believe that we will see countless innovative approaches to the religious life. These will be approaches of great appeal to our stakeholders, who will join with us in transforming our historical institutions.

The Metanoic Experience

As we approach the third millennium, only the incurably naive or the hopelessly myopic will not see a qualitatively radical shift of environment in the major economic and social institutions of the world. The impact on nations, organizations, and the people in them transcends the myths, metaphors, and models of our Traditional Paradigms. Changing beliefs, conflicting values, and cultural transformations are more than present within any particular nation; they are manifest in our "once-large, now turned globally-small" world (DeThomasis, 1988). The following four factors have precipitated this new world condition:

1. the disappearance of classical forms of industrial organization in favor of information-driven dynamics
2. the emergence of highly competitive concentrations of power in the oligopolies of global finance
3. the rise of large-scale, multinational organizations dependent upon no single nation state
4. a democratic revolution that has raised the aspirations of millions of men and women across the globe (DeThomasis, 1988)

These dynamics have raised several fundamental ethical issues. Who may earn even a subsistence level of living? Who may work with human dignity free of prejudice? Who may live on the land and take responsibility for stewardship over it? These issues of social justice face anyone who has a measure of control over the goods and services of modern society. And they bear most heavily on the consciousness of religious men and women who have the unique capacity to affect the decisions of the powerful as well as the life chances of the unfortunate.

If we, as concerned religious, are to take up this burden, we will not succeed if we must also carry the weight of the traditional religious life. We must transform our lives and organizations to accommodate global reality so that our energies can be directed at an ever-expanding apostolate. The Transformal Paradigm I am proposing is a framework on which new lives can be constructed—a radical shift of ground that has the potential to shake loose our imagination so that we will attract new vocations and experience a new vibrant life for our religious orders.

But the Transformal Paradigm is more than a modification of our rules and rituals. It is a metanoic experience that alters our spirituality and refocuses our commitment. As the word *metanoia* suggests, embracing the ideas underlying the Transformal Paradigm involves a fundamental shift of mind (Kiefer and Stroh, 1984). We no longer think of the religious life in the same terms. What was once a personal relationship between each of us and God, is now a network of social interactions in which spirituality brings God among us. What was once authoritative and doctrinaire is now negotiable and fluid. What was left to the will of God is now accepted as human responsibility.

In the chapters to follow, we will see how each dimension of the Transformal Paradigm shapes a new religious life. In these pages, the emphasis will be placed on the metanoic experience so that individual religious can clearly see the transformation required in their own beliefs and behavior. For it is in our individual metanoia that we find the spiritual energy and imagination needed to vitalize the religious life.

References

DeThomasis, L. (1987) *Faith, Finance and Society.* Memphis, TN: Christian Brothers College.

DeThomasis, L. (1988) *Monasteries on Wall Street? The Ten Commandments of Doing Ethics in Business.* Winona, MN: Saint Mary's College Publications.

Faller, J.M. (1990) *The At Risk Learner and the At Risk School.* Unpublished PhD thesis, University of Minnesota.

John Paul II. (1988) "Sollicitudo Rei Socialis," *National Catholic Reporter,* 24(31).

Kiefer, C., and Stroh, P. (1984) "A New Paradigm for Developing Organizations," in Adams, ed., *Transforming Work.* Alexandria, VA: Miles River Press.

Lakoff, G., and Johnson, M. (1980) *Metaphors We Live By.* Chicago: University of Chicago Press.

Miller, D. (1985) "Social Policy: An Exercise in Metaphor," *Knowledge: Creation, Diffusion, Utilization,* 7, 191–215.

Morgan, G. (1986) *Images of Organization.* Newbury Park, CA: Sage Publications.

Wheeler, C. (1987) "The Magic of Metaphor: A Perspective on Reality Construction," *Metaphor and Symbolic Activity,* 225–237.

CHAPTER 4

Transforming Ministry in Turbulent Times

DIMENSION	TRADITIONAL	TRANSFORMAL
PURPOSE	Apostolate/Ministry	Transformation

For most religious, the apostolate has been the centerpiece of their lives. Each of us has come to terms with the way our order has translated the ideas of a founder into specific guidelines for how we are to live and work. Most apostolates also specify who is to benefit from the good works of religious men and women. Thus, we have apostolates to the poor, to those who are ill, and others who are in need.

As I pointed out in Chapter 3, the traditional apostolate was an important concept in simpler times. In the distant past, those in need "stayed put"; their conditions rarely changed, the knowledge and skill of the religious person was relatively simple and stable, and the values and expectations of church and society did not vary in any significant way. In other words, the solutions to the problems of the needy were discoverable and could be forged into well-defined apostolates. Religious men and women truly knew what was best for their clients, and more importantly, they knew what needed to be done to improve the lives of those they served.

But these are not the Middle Ages—these are turbulent times when social change is sweeping the globe. Given the magnitude of changes in our clients and their needs, it is not surprising that the traditional apostolates and their associated ministries give little guidance to today's religious. This is not to say that our founders were wrong. Far from it. They were insightful men and women who perceived the human consequences of the societies of their time and designed inspired responses to correct abuse and inequity. The apostolates they passed down to us are wrong only when we fail to adapt them to the conditions and needs of those who are disadvantaged by contemporary society.

Ministering in Turbulent Times

When I took the title to this chapter from Peter Drucker's book *Managing In Turbulent Times,* I wanted to play off several of his key points (Drucker, 1980). First, I saw that his characterization of modern society as *turbulent* applied just as much to religious life as it did to business and commerce. Second, I wished to compare modern religious with managers in that we have a responsibility to shape our organizations to changed expectations and opportunities. Finally, I felt that we too are "market driven," and our clients have a good deal to say about how we are to use the gifts God has given us. When I consider these three parallels together, I have no trouble making a case for examining the concept of ministering in turbulent times. In my way of thinking, to do anything else would be to betray the charisma of countless founders.

As the title to this chapter suggests, we are called not to familiar ministries but to transformation. The distinction between these views of the apostolate is crucial to the message of this book. To minister to the needs of our clients so that they can adapt to the circumstances of their lives is surely among the highest goals of the religious life. However, by narrowly emphasizing our familiar ministries, we are blinded to the chaos fostered by social, economic and political turbulence. If we only minister, we are increasingly overwhelmed by the form and scope of our clients' need.

We must, instead, take a larger view of the environment in which our ministries play out—a view that cuts to the underlying turbulence and seeks to transform the forces that create the problems of our students, patients, and parishioners. If we fail to make this paradigm shift, we will be swamped by the demands of countless people in need whose misery will increase without limit as turbulence goes unchecked and unshaped. To accept the challenge of transformation is not as revolutionary as it first appears. Most religious orders were founded out of a perceived need to deal with societal turbulence, and their apostolic vision centered on transforming the conditions of life.

A critical reading of the history of any religious order will, I believe, support the conclusion that every founder was inspired by God to minister to the needs of those caught up in the turbulence of those times. Let's consider Saint John Baptist de La Salle as a case in point. When he founded the Christian Brothers, Saint La Salle did not ignore the economic, political, or moral-cultural conditions of seventeenth-century France. Instead, Saint La Salle proceeded with great care, concern, and pragmatic wisdom to found his religious community. It took him more than thirty years to introduce the pedagogical and school management changes of his new religious teaching community.

> Since no educational reform would have been possible without the agreement, at least tacit, of the notables, the elected town council, the bishop, the royal supervisor and, in the great cities, the leaders of parliament, it is easy to understand why De La Salle proceeded with such caution. (Aroz, et al., 1980)

With great faith in his religious calling, Saint La Salle interpreted the signs of his time. Blessed with grace, and with considerable human ingenuity, he translated his faith into a pragmatic program of service by mastering and manipulating the economic, political, and moral-cultural realities of his day.

If we consider the effect of Saint La Salle's educational model, we can clearly see that it transformed schooling. While each of his students was the beneficiary of his ministry, society and countless generations of students experienced an educational environment that resisted the forces of turbulence. Saint La Salle truly found his purpose in transformation.

Today, the life and vitality of the Christian Brothers, or of any religious community, depends upon how religious respond to the contemporary world. In the spirit of each founder, the community must read the signs of the times. However, these signs must be read through a lens of reality that does not let social turbulence distort the vision of the founder. To do this effectively, the community must utilize the economic, political, and moral-cultural dynamics at work in modern society. Only through such a re-examination of purpose can religious communities find the levers of control whereby they can transform social, economic, and political realities.

It is the message and spirit of transformation, not the details and specifics of an ancient apostolate, that is as relevant today as it was in the distant past. The details and specifics can always be worked out by taking a pragmatic approach to the turbulence we see around us. For example, the essence of the Gospel message lies not in specific actions such as Jesus' multiplication of the loaves and fishes, or the casting out of the demons, or the calming of the seas. If these specifics are the essence of the message, religious communities would surely be in great difficulty today. The essence of the message is, of course, love. And it is love that is as vitally needed today as it was two thousand years ago—or will be two thousand years hence. The message transcends the constraints of time and the pragmatic circumstances of the moment. It calms turbulence and lets the peace and promise of the Gospel flow to those immersed in seas of change.

The question we face today is "How can religious transform their apostolates into vital ministries?" I believe this question can be partitioned into three components that can help us see the root causes of the ministerial challenges of today. These components are what Drucker would call the *New Realities* (1989): the economic, political, and moral-cultural frame in which we must find our purpose and the means to achieve it. I see this as a set of "ministries," each closely linked to a corresponding "reality," in which religious find pragmatic ways to transform society.

Ministering to Economic Reality

For centuries economists, political philosophers, and social reformers have debated the relationship between economy and society. In the last several decades, these discussions have been popularized so that nearly every man and woman in the world is aware that there are (or were) two fundamental ways of organizing economic activity. Socialism and capitalism were in open competition in every region of the world and measured their relative performance by the calculus of military and political power.

Now that socialism, in its Marxist-Leninist version, has failed, it is only natural to conclude that capitalism has won the debate and is the legitimate economic and political force of the future. While this may be a fair conclusion in the short run, I believe forces at work could call it into question in the years ahead. I am inclined to agree with Robert Heilbroner when he says, "Just because socialism has lost does not mean that capitalism has won" (1991, p. 130).

What I'm worried about are some alarming trends in the world economy that are increasing human misery and the need for new, transformed ministries. Before I spell out these developments, let me say that I am a confirmed capitalist. But I recognize that capitalism too has unacceptable social consequences that cannot be tolerated. These are always lurking at the margins when self-interest takes precedence over social concern. These are forces that must be balanced if the benefits of economic activity are to be widely shared in any social order. As Pope John Paul II states in *Centesimus Annus,*

The social order will be all the more stable, the more it does not place in opposition personal interest and the interests of society as a whole, but rather seeks ways to bring them into fruitful harmony. (1991, p. 17)

I am sorry to say that the balance between personal gain and social benefit is very much out of line in every country today. The effects of imbalance are very much in evidence in the following realities.

Shrinking Work Opportunity: The driving force of any modern society grows out of the contributions of working men and women. To the extent that there is wide opportunity to work, economies grow and standards of living rise. When opportunity shrinks, growth stagnates and people everywhere are worse off. Problematic in modern capitalism is the worker base, which is shrinking in all industrialized countries. Automation of production and the migration of manufacturing to Third World countries means fewer jobs on the capitalist flagships. At the same time, with these newly created jobs, human beings are exploited and treated as cheap, disposable labor. In the Third World, these jobs enhance urbanization, which cannot be sustained, and destroy family systems, which cannot be replaced.

It's very clear to me that the individual–society balance has tipped toward self-interest. Too few people control decisions that affect too many, and they use their power to widen the gap between those who have and those who are in despair. If we are to fashion a credible, useful ministry that takes economic reality into account, this is the gap that we must help to close.

In the past, we have generally worked with people to help them jump the gap between the "haves" and the "have nots." When a person couldn't make the jump, we were at hand to ease suffering and, when possible, prepare the person for another try. In my view, this was at the center of our apostolates.

Clearly, we could continue to provide the apostolic support of the past. However, the scale of human misery in the modern world makes even our best efforts seem insignificant. No matter how many children we educate, homeless we house, and sick we comfort, their numbers continue to grow beyond our capacity to respond. We need a ministry that addresses the causes of misery and uses the talents of religious men and women to ameliorate their effects. We must assess our ability to influence economic systems and target our energy and resources where they will do the most good. I believe that transformed capitalism can energize us again by recognizing that we all have mutual interests that must be served so that large elements of society no longer feel alienated and dispossessed (De-Thomasis, 1992).

Failed Life Support Systems: Today the world's economies are increasingly involved in manipulating peoples' perceptions and tastes rather than in meeting their basic needs. Instead of economies directed at feeding and housing those in need, we have systems of production and marketing that accumulate resources for the rich. The net result is that the world's life support systems are failing.

All persons in positions of influence and power must bear some of the responsibility for these failed systems. They have measured economies against standards of growth rather than measures of participation. They have calculated their profits without accounting for the misery of millions. And they have lost sight of their own humanity.

Hunger is the measure of the failure of economic systems. Most of us know that we are in precarious times when the world may not be able feed its population. This must be the first priority for economic development, and we must hold our economic systems accountable when anyone goes hungry.

Unfaithful Stewards: The human consequences of misdirected economic systems seem almost insignificant compared to the environmental damage bill. This bill is so large and has been accounted so many times that many leaders have come to take its depressing bottom line for granted. Their response is that of the unfaithful steward who says, "I will take and use these resources. Let the unborn generations worry about the consequences."

The way we run our economic systems enhances the pressure people put on their environments. Scarce resources will be used up. Living space is polluted. Mankind will become the only species remaining in a biologically-devastated world. These are conditions that we can no longer tolerate—our environment is telling us that there isn't much time to take up the demands of stewardship. But how do we, as a few religious, have any impact on these global systems? How can we create an economic ministry that can transform economic activity?

The primary resources we can use to further the goals of an economic ministry are religious men and women. Most of us are highly trained in the professions and experienced in organizing and managing social institutions. These are skills that can readily be channeled to influence corporations, governments and social service agencies. To use these skills, religious will need to see themselves as managers and economic decision makers—as transformers, taking on executive roles in corporations and becoming political leaders. As they do so, they will spread the good news of their ministry and enlist others to its cause.

The church and religious organizations also possess considerable economic power. They have money to invest, and through investment they can transform economic policies that affect tens of thousands of people. By aggregating their resources and voting their stock, religious can intervene in economic activities to create opportunity.

But what about the argument that religious should be poor and serve the poor? After all, isn't this a central tenet of most apostolates? Shouldn't we spend our money to feed and house those in need?

I firmly believe that these questions must be answered with a ministry that engages in the economy rather than in mopping up the social spills the economy creates. We must become participants in economic reality and transform our paradigm of religious life so that it supports religious men and women as they become influential actors in shaping that reality to serve all people.

Ministering to Political Reality

If we characterize the current economic reality as *turbulent,* it's easy to label political reality as *chaotic.* Throughout the world, political systems are undergoing fundamental changes, and new constellations of power are emerging almost daily. Yet within this apparent chaos, several trends will be shaping the political reality of the future. It is the human consequences following on these trends that have important implications for our ministries. Here is how I see the challenges we face in the emerging political reality.

Bureaucratic Power: Every political reality has its bureaucratic infrastructure. Political decisions are funneled through agencies whose administrative laws determine how citizens are affected by policy. These bureaucracies are necessary to track the course of policy, but they stifle creativity and subordinate humanity to the whims of the state. As Carnoy and Samoff see it,

> . . . tendencies toward bureaucracy, hierarchy and *dirigisme* gradually reduce the capability of the state to mobilize citizens to innovate

and re-energize society. The reduction of commitment and activism tends to produce a new individualism where workers draw guaranteed material and social benefits from the collective but channel their creative energy into defending themselves against the collective or into defining an individual space for overcoming collective inefficiency. This separation of the creative, active individual from the collective deadens collective action and makes social renovation difficult. (1990, p. 373)

These are the political dynamics that have set creative individuals like Lech Walesa and Vaclav Havel against their governments. That these men were effective in helping to transform political reality overlooks the thousands of others whose creativity was stifled. Bureaucratic systems are necessary to the operation of modern governments, but they are neither sufficient to meeting human needs, nor can they reform themselves. These are the ministerial challenges that we and other concerned people must take up. By engaging and transforming bureaucracy and helping governments speak to the real needs of people, the political ministry can help to make the relationship between bureaucracy and citizens one of productive adaptation rather than cynical confrontation.

Democracy and Aspiration: The explosion of democratic movements across the globe can be taken as an expression of human desires to have a voice in the decisions shaping the future. Electronic communication has created an informed population in every nation—a population whose aspirations for a better life becomes focused on the political process. In the minds of those who press for democracy, there is a simple equation: political voice results in increased standards of living.

We have already seen that this equation is faulty in that it does not recognize the lag between political reform and social results. The unhappy truth—now being played out in the former communist empire—is that democracy often makes conditions worse in the short run. When President Yeltsin argued for free prices and the economic reforms that equate to democracy, he recognized that "things will have to get worse in order to get better" (1991). If nations do not find ways to respond to the aspiration gap, democratic movements can soon turn to revolutionary means. The challenge to the political ministry is a complex one. We must educate both political actors and citizens in the workings of the democratic process and help them to shape their aspirations to realistic levels.

Political Debate Versus Armed Confrontation: All of the above economic and political dynamics are at work in a world where armaments are used as instruments of debate. The industrial countries of the world have engaged in an irresponsible production and marketing of arms so that literally every person has the means to kill. I once heard it said that if the destructive power of the world's armaments were apportioned to each man, woman, and child, we would each own forty barrels of TNT!

We usually think of armed conflict as something that governments do to one another or that terrorists do to us. This perspective clouds the issue, for it is what we can now do to one another that makes political debate less and less likely, Even children are armed and dangerous. In a recent study, the National Center for Disease Control found that twenty percent of American high school students carry weapons on a given day (*Education Week,* 1991). Our schools and our cities are armed camps where violence is the norm.

The challenge to our political ministry is twofold. We must be convincing advocates of nonviolence and help our clients to see that problems can be solved without physical force. But we must also be a voice of rationality in the political arena to reduce—if not eliminate—the proliferation of weapons.

Ministering to Cultural Reality

Although the dynamics of economic and political life have wrought great changes in the human condition in recent times, there has been even greater turmoil in the moral-cultural dimension. Western societies have lost their grip on culture and taken on a superficial, media-defined view of the meaning of the human condition. At the same time, underdeveloped nations are experiencing a revival of cultural identity that intensifies religious interest and intolerance. These are new realities that we must understand and engage if we are to carry the morality of Christ into the next millennium.

Western Cultural Poverty: Let me first define what we are talking about. I see culture as an integration of "(1) Systems of ideas or beliefs . . . (2) Systems of expressive symbols; for instance, art forms and styles . . . (3) Systems of value orientations . . ." where the emphasis is on integration (Parsons and Shils, 1962, p. 8). That is, all ideas, symbols, and values "hang together," and they are agreed upon by the vast majority of people who are immersed in the culture. In addition, this integrated set of perceptions can be transmitted by families and schools so that there is generational integrity to the thoughts and actions of people.

If you read this definition closely, it's easy to see why Western societies are culturally impoverished. Let me explore this one point at a time. First, there is no consensus on what we believe. Each group, and often each group member, has unique beliefs about the workings of society. We can see this writ large in the domestic debate over handguns. The National Rifle Association believes that "guns don't kill people—people kill people." But the mothers of slain teenagers know that "guns kill." In this example, there is no consensus on the ways humans use tools, and the culture (if it can be called that) is fragmented in its search for a workable social policy.

Second, in the case of expressive symbols few cultural norms exist. Instead, we experience a veritable blizzard of symbols, each with a short life that is defined by its reception in the popular media. Thus, when the rich cast off their designer clothes, the needy may not accept them if they have the wrong label. The result is that there is no way for people to work out their own identity in the symbols of the times; they are too fluid to serve as an anchor to character.

Finally, it is in the area of values that Western societies are most gravely at risk. There has been a total paradigm shift that has thrown over standards of humanity in favor of the expedient. This is at the root of policies that can foment war to test weapons with one hand and fail to respond to the human wreckage of war with the other. It also underlies the crises of leadership, which has no beacons to guide our organizations, and the rot at the center of our communities and families.

The grave danger to humanity posed by Western cultural poverty is this. When boundless economic and political powers are able to proceed without the benefit of cultural guidance, they can do immense harm to the human condition. Here is the challenge to religious men and women. Can we help to reverse the cultural decay by articulating the Christian message with the dynamics of modern society? I believe that we can, but only if we minister to the true moral-cultural realities of our times and transform the orientation of our social, economic, and political systems to create rather than destroy.

Third World Cultural Rediscovery: While Western societies are losing their cultural roots, people in the Third World are rediscovering theirs. In the impoverished nations, we find new interest in religion and demands that governments be responsive to the needs of people. In effect, these people are crying out against the injustice of modernity. They long for a village-centered life where culture shaped interactions and gave meaning to all activity.

I believe that the people of the Third World have something very important to say to us. They are essentially in agreement with Christopher Alexander in his prescription for cultural integrity.

> Wherever possible, work toward the evolution of independent regions in the world; each with a population between 2 and 10 million; each with its own economy; each one autonomous and self-governing; each with a seat in a world government, without the intervening power of larger states or countries. (1977, p. 14)

Such an ideal world would give free play to the cultural differences among people. It would also stand in the way of bitter nationalistic rivalries and the bloodshed that invariably accompanies them. For it is this side of the Third World cultural rediscovery that is the most dangerous to our futures. It is tempting to see the demands of these peoples for autonomy and independence as positive indicators of the victory of democracy over communism. But there is a dark side, as Gaddis points out.

> But the forces of fragmentation do not just take the form of pressures for self-determination, formidable though those may be. They also show up in the field of economics, where they manifest themselves as protectionism: the effort, by various means, to insulate individual economies from the tension that can develop, both among states and within them. . . They certainly show up in the area of religion. The resurgence of Islam might be seen by some as an integrationist force in the Middle East. But it is surely fragmentationist to the extent that it seeks to set that particular region off from the rest of the world. . . ." (1991, p. 106)

If the world is not to degenerate into small, warring camps, we at the centers of economic and political power must find ways to recognize cultural differences while emphasizing the cultural integrity of humanity. There is no higher priority. We must learn to live together, or we will surely destroy the human fabric.

Transforming Purpose

The paradigm shift called for in the above paragraphs is one that moves from witness to action. In our traditional apostolates, we were largely engaged in bearing witness to the message of Christ. Although we did countless good works and lightened the burdens of innumerable unfortunates, it was our witness that influenced others to consider how they too might benefit those in need.

If we accept the challenge of a new ministry of transformation, we are committing ourselves to action. We are saying that religious will walk the corridors of power and directly influence the decisions that affect the lives of the powerless. By taking up this new purpose, we are becoming an integral part of the solution to human problems. This is the essence of the transformed purpose.

PURPOSE: RELIGIOUS MEN AND WOMEN ARE ENGAGED IN THE MINISTRY OF ACTION. THEY ARE ACTIVELY INVOLVED IN MAKING ECONOMIC, POLITICAL, AND MORAL DECISIONS BY WHICH THEY DEFINE THE MESSAGE OF CHRIST IN THE HUMAN CONSEQUENCES OF WHAT THEY DO

References

Alexander, C. et al. (1977) *A Pattern Language.* New York: Oxford University Press.

Aroz, L. et al. (1980) *Beginnings: De La Salle and His Brothers.* (Salm, ed.) Romeoville, IL: Christian Brothers Publications.

Carnoy, M., and Samoff, J. (1990) *Education and Social Transition in the Third World.* Princeton, NJ: Princeton University Press.

DeThomasis, L. (1992) "New World Emerging in Europe, and the U.S. Can't Stand Still," *Minneapolis Star Tribune.* Minneapolis, MN: March 7, p. 13A.

Drucker, P. (1980) *The New Realities.* New York: Harper and Row.

Education Week (1991) "20 Percent of High School Students Carry Weapons," October 16, p. 8.

Gaddis, J. (1991) "Toward the Post-Cold War World," *Foreign Affairs,* 70 (2), 102–122.

Heilbroner, R. (1991) "Just Because Socialism Has Lost Does Not Mean That Capitalism Has Won," *Forbes,* May 27, pp. 130–135.

John Paul II. (1991) "Centesimus Annus," *Origins,* 21 (1), 1–24.

Parsons, T., and Shils, E. (1962) *Toward a General Theory of Action.* New York: Harper and Row.

Yeltsin, B. (1991) *Address To the Russian Parliament.* Moscow, USSR, October 28.

CHAPTER 5

The Transformation of Control

DIMENSION		TRADITIONAL	TRANSFORMAL
CONTROL		Congregation	Stakeholders

The Traditional Paradigm of congregational control is based on an assumption of stability. In this view the world changes slowly, the needs of our clients remain the same, and others see us in historical perspective. The coincidence of these several perceptions makes it possible for us to decide, as a congregation, how to live our lives and where to direct our apostolic work.

It is my contention that the views of our reference groups are no longer in agreement. Some in the church see our work from a traditional point of view and continue to emphasize the apostolic nature of our work. In contrast, the members of our congregations have widely divergent ideas as to the purpose and direction of religious life, so much so that collegial debate often degenerates into political wrangling as we decide our future. The same can be said of our clients. They are a heterogeneous group with divergent needs and values: their needs become ever greater and their demands more compelling each day.

To these three stakeholders (church, congregations, and clients), I would add a fourth—that of the *ecology* of human life on this planet. We are no longer immune from the consequences of our lifestyles, and we are becoming ever more aware that each of our actions must be evaluated as to its impact on the ecology around us. The realities I described in Chapter 4 are specific instances of the impact of social ecology on religious communities.

The Church and the People of God

The fragmentation of interests of our stakeholders creates a set of pressures on each congregation. We can visualize these forces in a simple diagram like that in Figure 5.1.

FIGURE 5.1

THE CHURCH AND THE PEOPLE OF GOD

THE PEOPLE OF GOD

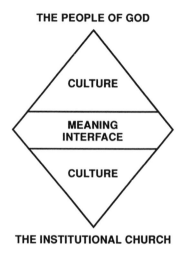

THE INSTITUTIONAL CHURCH

The conflict among our stakeholders is founded in their specific cultural contexts and surfaces when they attempt to give meaning to religious activities. At this "meaning interface," issues of control must be resolved and cultural compromises must be reached.

Some want conformity to a traditional apostolic purpose. This is purpose that draws on its historical interpretation of Christian culture to support a hierarchy of authority that controls the work of religious and their ministry to the people of God. Our clients, the people of God, attach their own meanings to the documents, norms, and values of the Christian culture. These often take the form of specific demands for services and support from religious men and women. What happens when these cultures interact is a dynamic definition of the living church (DeThomasis, 1984).

It is important to understand that Figure 5.1 represents the church in its totality. Our Catholic tradition teaches that the hierarchy, or institutional church comprised of clergy, Curia, and dioceses, is not the totality of the church. Moreover, Figure 5.1 suggests that no single party to this interaction defines totally on its own what the living church is to be. The church is the real, living dialogue and dynamism of a continually evolving search for meaning. It is only through a free search for meaning that we can say that the church is alive and well.

It is also important to note that our faith teaches that the church cannot exist apart from the people of God. In fact, it is only through the people that the church becomes a vital institution. The dynamics of this situation, which can only be described as the true mystery of the church, are based on the following observations.

1. Flowing from the people of God in their process of self-actualization come their various expressions of meaning (Maslow, 1968). Related church organizations, liturgical celebrations, and forms of spirituality emanate from the people of God in support of the people of God. It is from the experiences and expressions of the people that the institutional church receives its reason for being.

2. God's revelations to the people, through the process of self-actualization as a community of Christian believers formed and united by the spirit of Jesus Christ, become actual to the degree that their faith is expressed in meanings. These meanings are captured by the magisterium in the scripture, dogma, revelation, liturgy, forms of spirituality, and related organizations as they are expressed in the context of the institutional church. Thus, the church is energized by the meanings assigned to these symbols and behaviors by the people. Neither the church nor the people of God can exist alone; each depends upon the other to define the meaning of the Christian experience.

3. Therefore, there will always be a tension (hopefully, one that is creative and constructive) between the people and the institutional church. Each will attempt to contribute to a shared meaning of the mystery of Christ.

4. This mystery will be a creative tension for the church insofar as the institutional church stands at the foundation point of the forces diagrammed in Figure 5.1. In its foundational role, the church draws heavily on the meanings defined by the people and uses its strength to support and serve them.

5. Debilitating tension occurs when the institutional church views itself as the only arbiter of the search for meaning.

6. Instead of dictating meaning to the people of God, the church, as an integral part of the mystery, must be responsive in a truly sensitive manner in the exercise of its role as the magisterium. Any static, dictatorial structure that cuts off dialogue and interaction among the people of God is always problematic in a context that proclaims Jesus Christ as the center of life. For Christ, who was himself both God and human, unites a church that is both sacred and secular through the mystery of his love.

Through the integration of the sacred and the secular, religious and other people of God can come to an understanding of the mystery and define meanings that breathe life into the church. Look again at Figure 5.1. As you travel from the point "The People of God," by whichever side of the triangle you choose, you arrive at the same baseline, the "Meaning Interface," while covering the perimeter of the space labeled "Culture." Now travel down either side and you arrive at the point "Institutional Church," while covering the perimeter of the second "Culture" space. The purpose of this journey is to make the point that the church is one. For the love of Christ to come into fruition, the people of God must reveal God's communication of that love in society: *through* the means by which the culture makes the communication possible; *with* the expressions of that love that the people of God make real through their liturgies and symbols; and *in* the loving service provided by the institutional church.

Meanings, Paradigms, and Models

What I am calling for in the above paragraphs is the identification and implementation of a new paradigm that will define the church for the people of God. This paradigm is rooted in the fundamental mythology of Christ. What we as stakeholders must do is find new metaphors and models whereby the charism of Jesus can vitalize the church and our own lives.

I am using *mythology* here in its deepest, spiritual sense. Christ is *mythical* in the sense that we cannot make an empirical test of his existence and his totality of truth as the Son of God. We can, however, test and verify the power of his message and love in everything we do. If we allow the power of love free rein, we can become part of the myth and use this power to energize the church and its work.

So it is not the mythical foundation of our paradigm that needs changing. It is the metaphor and the associated models that are out of date. I see the need for new metaphors and models as control issues, because the old model of the church is no longer received by most as an embodiment of mythical power. Instead it persists as a rigid structure, a model that prevents the people of God from realizing the promise of Christ in today's era of changing paradigms. Thus, the primary task is to create a new metaphor of the church and a working model of religious activity in which control can be shared among all stakeholders. This is what I have in mind in Figure 5.1 when I emphasize the importance of the Meaning Interface.

Very well then, how can the people of God carry out a successful search for new metaphors and models? If we let them alone, it seems clear that many could forsake the institutional church and thus destroy the essence of the magisterium, an essential faith-filled element of the total reality of what is the church. As they wander free, many will despair of finding meaningful paradigms that speak to the immediate concerns of their lives. Others are likely to come together in small groups or sects where they find others whose metaphors speak to them. These are the consequences of centuries-long emphases on the model of the church.

While the straying of the people of God from the institutional church may meet the needs of some, it weakens the living church. Individuals and sects do not share metaphors—to say nothing of models—and the love of Christ is diffused rather than focused. This is entropy at work (Katz and Kahn, 1978). The church as a social system is running down and will eventually be a minor player on the world scene, unless it is re-vitalized with powerful, meaningful metaphors.

While I cannot presume to supply the metaphor, I believe that ways exist to discover meanings that will appeal to the needs of the people of God. My sense of the future of the church is that vital metaphors reside in the minds of the people, and it is our task as religious to help them emerge. If we become informed interpreters of the ecology to the people, we can be the instruments whereby a new paradigm emerges.

Congregations and the Ecology of Religious Life

To see how religious congregations can be involved in the search for a new paradigm, let me add to Figure 5.1. Here, I show that "meaning" is, in reality, the set of myths, metaphors, and models used to articulate the church with the people of God. If shared meaning is to unite the people, it must embrace all three aspects of paradigms. Hence, we must all focus on how we can translate the myth of Christ and the reality of his existence into popular metaphors and, ultimately, into the model that will re-vitalize the church.

By putting "congregation" at one end of the meaning interface and "ecology" at the other, I intend to challenge religious men and women. I am suggesting that they become the instruments whereby new forms of effective stakeholder contributions to the church become reality. In control in the past, we now set the signposts of issues that the people of God must address as they seek to develop a model of the church in which they have a constructive and meaningful influence.

FIGURE 5.2

THE SEARCH FOR CONTROLLING PARADIGMS

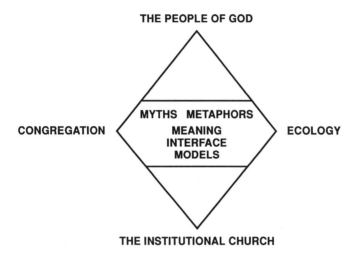

Figure 5.2 introduces a new player into the traditional view of religious activity. While the ecology is not an active player, it is more compelling; it defines our options and the consequences that flow from them. When we consider how these forces bear on a congregation that is no longer of one mind, we can see that control of religious organizations is no simple matter. Let me give an example.

In many, if not most, of the writings concerning the future of the church, I find religious leaders waffling on the major social issues of the times. Consider the facts of population growth. In 1968, world population was approximately 3.5 billion. In just over twenty years, that number has grown to 5.3 billion and will clearly result in a doubling (to 7 billion) by the year 2000 (Ehrlich and Ehrlich, 1990). If we assume that all this started with Adam and Eve, we will reach that 7 billion with just 32 doublings. (If you doubt this, just work it out on your pocket calculator.) And as demographers point out, "Filling all of the land surface of the planet Earth to the density of Manhattan would take us to only 10 more doublings from where we are now" (Keyfitz, 1977, p. 9). But we won't have the option of ten more. In the last twenty years, more than 200 million persons have died of hunger and disease. Most of these were children. Fourteen million children died of health-related causes in 1988. Most of these were Third World children, victims of the dual pressures of population growth and limited agricultural production (United Nations, 1988).

In response to the human misery imposed by our reaching of ecological limits, the church has indeed waffled on the question of population control. It has failed Third World parents, not because of our teachings on birth control but because it has applied Western remedies to countries without the economic systems necessary to deal with the health and medical needs of parents and children so that they may be reasonably positioned to put into effect the moral teachings of our church regarding birth control. And we religious have been but bystanders in the social policy debates of nations lest we become too involved in secular matters. This sort of unreal detachment must stop! The proof of this conclusion lies in the alarming numbers of people who are turning from the church. These are good people who want guidance and directions to help solve problems and reduce misery so that they can remain faithful to the magisterium of the church.

Those of us in religious congregations must grasp issues such as population growth, hunger, and social injustice and become effective strategic planners to help the people of God within the historical church. We must help people seek answers to these survival questions. How else can we assist them in attaining the state of self-actualization? Remember, when Maslow proposed self-actualization as the highest of a hierarchy of human needs, he founded his structure on safety and security (Maslow, 1968). If the people of God cannot meet their basic needs for survival, there is no way that they will be able to eat of the bread of life offered by the church and live according to the magnificent and loving values espoused by a church faithful to the Gospel message.

Now, I'm going to break my promise not to propose a metaphor—I do have one in mind. Suppose we think of the church as a safety net. Let it help the people of God deal with the fundamental issues of their lives. Let it help them climb the hierarchy of needs toward self-actualization. But let it be a safety net that can catch them should they lose hold on their climb.

A wonderful example that comes to mind of the church as safety net is the House of Loaves and Fishes in Duluth, Minnesota. This is a home for homeless people run by members of the Catholic Worker Movement. It is truly a safety net in that homeless people can come to a shelter to live as members of a family and use the support of committed men, women, and children to get back on their climb toward self-actualization.

This example is especially relevant for a transformed church. Note that the House of Loaves and Fishes is not operated by religious. Instead, it is the Catholic Worker Movement that is providing the safety net; a group that has been historically at the margins of the institutional church. There is another side to Loaves and Fishes. These people of God make the argument that America could house and feed all of its homeless with a fraction of its defense expenditures. They are taking action to gain a political voice that might, one day, redress the social policies of this country.

Where, my brothers and sisters, were we? Where are the loaves and fishes needed by the people we serve? And where is the church in taking action to provide a safety net? The answer is, I'm afraid, *nowhere!* We have failed to help those in need to control their lives. We have permitted the relationship of the people to their personal ecologies to deteriorate. In the misery that invariably results, the people turn to other paradigms and meanings or give up in despair. Is it any wonder that we fail to get sufficient vocations to the religious life today?

We should not conclude from the above discussion that we should give up hope of bringing order to what we do. It does mean, however, that we must view control and decision-making in a new light, one that will show both the bright and dark sides of our life and work. I believe we can in fact shed some light on this problem by considering just what is meant by stakeholder control under the safety net metaphor.

Stakeholders and Control of Religious Organizations

Let's try one more version of our drawing, Figure 5.3. Think of the interactions we've been talking about as the four corners of a safety net.

In this use of the safety net metaphor, it's as if the four stakeholders are manning a net that must be moved to catch those who fall through the cracks in society. Just as a fire company might act, the stakeholders must coordinate their movements so the net is ready to save the person in need. If one stakeholder pulls too hard, the net will shift off center, and the needy will suffer. If all pull too hard, the net will break, and there will be no help for the victims of social and economic circumstance. And, most importantly, if no stakeholder pulls at all, the net will be but a flabby attempt at saving the unfortunate. These are, I believe, the essential principles of stakeholder control.

Does this mechanistic view of control mean that God has been left out of the governance of our affairs? I don't think so. In fact, the fundamen-

73

FIGURE 5.3

CONTROLLING THE SAFETY NET

THE PEOPLE OF GOD

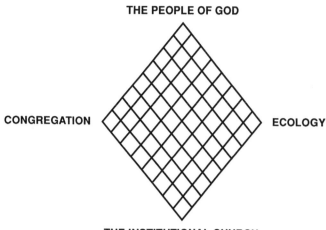

CONGREGATION

ECOLOGY

THE INSTITUTIONAL CHURCH

tal liturgical truth, "Through him, with him, and in him, all glory and honor is yours, Almighty Father, forever and ever!" is inherent in the interactions that vitalize the safety net of the church.

How is this so? First, through the communications among the people of God, our congregations, and the institutional church, we define the ecological reality in which we live. Through our interactions, we identify those in need and the services and support that will lighten their burdens.

Second, with the love of the people and congregations, the church is vitalized to reach out to those in need.

Finally, in the loving relationship established among all the people, the Gospel of Christ is realized. In effect God the Father has re-established an institutional church *through* Jesus Christ, *with* the power of the Holy Spirit as revealed *in* the people of God. Thus, it is the totality of all stakeholders in their ecology that defines the church.

To confuse the living church with the institutional church—as we have invariably done in the past—is the result of seeing the church only as an institution. Even the hierarchical church does not want us to see it in such a confined view. By perceiving the living church as a manifestation of the love of Christ, we see at once a unified expression of God in reality. As Paul Ricoeur writes:

The Fathers knew that Man is one and many, the individual and the collectivity; man is each man and all mankind. Some of them were aware that Adam meant Man, Anthropos, not an old individual gentleman, all alone with his wife in a garden, who would transmit his quite individual and personal propensity for evil to his descendants by means of physical generation. They were capable of conceiving a singular collective, an individual who had the value of an entire nation, collectivity, convertible into individual thoughts, volitions, and feelings. They always understood this paradox because they had retained the historical and cosmic dimensions of the image of God. (1965, pp. 112–113)

This quotation tells us that the people of God are at once all people, each individual, and the personification of God. By accepting this fundamental and timeless truth, we are acknowledging the right of stakeholders to be a vital and integral part of the church. Due to the pivotal role of religious congregations in the living church, we too come under the sway of stakeholder interests and must engage in the debates over our purpose and the ways we will use the resources God has given us. This is the foundation for a new perspective on control.

CONTROL: ALL STAKEHOLDERS ARE INVOLVED IN DEFINING THE ORGANIZING PARADIGM FOR A LIVING CHURCH—ONE THAT ENERGIZES PEOPLE TO PURSUE SELF-ACTUALIZATION AND PROVIDES A SAFETY NET FOR THOSE WHO FALTER IN THEIR QUEST.

References

DeThomasis, L. (1984) *My Father's Business: Creating a New Future for the People of God*. Westminster, MD: Christian Classics.

Ehrlich, P., and Ehrlich, A. (1990) *The Population Explosion*. New York: Simon and Schuster.

Katz, D., and Kahn, D. (1978) *The Social Psychology of Organizations*. New York: J. Wiley.

Keyfitz, N. (1977) *Applied Mathematical Demography*. New York: J. Wiley.

Maslow, A. (1968) *Toward A Psychology of Being*. New York: Van Nostrand.

Ricoeur, P. (1965) *History and Truth*. Evanston, IL: Northwestern University Press.

CHAPTER 6

The Social Ecology of Religious Organization

DIMENSION		TRADITIONAL	TRANSFORMAL
MODE OF ORGANIZATION		Bureaucracy	Symbiotic

Men and women build walls around their organizations in order to control what goes on inside. When they do so, they intentionaily isolate themselves from their environments and permit only selective exchanges with the people and other organizations around them.

These two simple sentences have shaped our thinking about organizational life since the invention of the medieval bureaucracy. Separation of organization and environment has been one of the basic attributes of business and social enterprise. Organization walls have made the modern corporation possible and have enabled the church to forge a worldwide network of controlled activity. The existence of these walls has given each of us a sanctuary in which the concerns of the world can be shut out, and we can attend to business and religion as defined within our corporations and cloisters.

In the case of the church, the separation of its activities from the world has influenced the ways religious men and women think about their lives. They cannot help but be influenced by a sacred-secular dualism that is, I believe, at the center of the traditional paradigm of the religious life. While we are beginning to observe an official rejection of such fragmented thinking, the grip of dualism persists in the models and metaphors that govern religious life. Although the church has denounced dualism in its doctrinal teachings, it has not managed to avoid its influence on the daily lives of religious and many of the people of God. For instance, the regulation of the Roman church on celibacy for priests, although grounded in principle, must not be tainted by the notion that priests, as ministers of the divine, ought to be divorced from their sexuality—as if God had not created men and women in their sexual form.

The tendency to build modern religious life on a dualistic foundation, placing spiritual and secular lives on two opposite poles, is firmly rooted in our subconscious. Because the tendency remains a feature of our mental models of religious life, it is embedded in the infrastructure of the church, affecting the activities and thoughts of thousands of the faithful. Unconscious dualism effectively impedes any attempts to move the church and religious institutions toward real, productive interactions with the modern world. Dualism stands in direct opposition to engagement with global society and to the changes in organizational forms that carry our ministries to those in need (DeThomasis, 1984).

If the church is to maintain its vitality and holiness into the twenty-first century, church leaders must become conscious of the dualism that infects and inhibits their vision of what they may or may not do. In the light of deeper truths, the church has no valid grounds for its reluctance to become fully incarnated in the world of pragmatic action. If it is to be true to the great truths of the Incarnation and the Resurrection—truths that utterly reject any dichotomy between the divine and the human, between spirit and nature, between religion and life—the church must thoroughly perceive these truths as a mandate to understand and relinquish its present reluctance to deal with worldly concerns within a sacred church.

Fortunately, many signposts point to paradigm change within the church. Take, for instance, Bishop Hubbard's address of 1983 in which he states:

> One effect of the renewal of the church, formally initiated with Vatican Council II, has been a blurring of the division between the sacred and the secular that had been so much part of our thinking as the church pursued its course in attempting to implement the mission committed to it by Jesus. With this blurring of the division, we have come to appreciate the interpenetration of the sacred and the secular . . . we have gained a renewed recognition that while the church is not of this world, it is indeed in this world. (1983, p. 731)

But debate alone, no matter how erudite and sensible, cannot tear down the walls we have constructed around the religious life. We have built these brick by brick and chinked them so that they are impenetrable to social reality. It is not only dualism that must go; the architecture that insulates religious men and women from their missions must be torn down and replaced by organizational forms that bring church and people into symbiotic relationship.

Symbiosis and the Religious Organism

The choice of the word *symbiosis* to describe the transformed religious organization grows naturally (if you will forgive the pun) from the ecological metaphor introduced in Chapter 3. The concept of *ecological symbiosis* helps us to understand how a new mode of organization can be established to foster the flows of human energy between religious and those they serve. Symbiosis breaks down the walls around the life to energize our missions with new recruits, increased resources, and eager clients. It addresses, in effect, all the major weaknesses of the Traditional Paradigm.

We can see symbiosis at work in many evolving forms of religious work and life. The school in the slums of New York that Sister Jean transformed is living testimony to the power of a symbiotic relationship between organization and environment. Her school is permeable to the many cultures around it, sensitive to the very different metaphors that shape the lives of its students, and engaged in the political and economic exchanges that make it a player in the educational system of the city. It is symbiotic with all the major actors in its environment.

Due to the symbiosis of its daily life, Sister Jean's school has a fluidity of form and adaptability of function that is at odds with the traditional paradigm of Catholic schooling. Many times, classroom instruction must take second place to the crises experienced by students. Rigid work schedules must be thrown over to accommodate the survival needs of children who are hungry, angry, and abused by their families and communities. Hierarchical management must give way to empowerment of frontline teachers, who must make critical decisions moment by moment. Like any surviving biological entity, Sister Jean's school must adapt or die. But more significantly, by adapting and creating a symbiotic relationship with its environment it not only survives, it thrives!

Although we usually talk about symbiosis in terms of the relationship between organization and environment, it is in the internal workings of the organization that symbiosis is readily observed in action. Symbiosis begins at home, where the organization and the people who work and live in it have the exchanges that define their mutual vitality. In the past, religious organizations have treated brothers, sisters, and clients as interchangeable parts. One person was seen as much like any other, and any individual could play a well-defined, standard role. This was not symbiosis. It was, instead, a procrustean bed that cut the individual to fit the organizational mold. Hence, it is not surprising that our vocations have fallen off, and clients have turned elsewhere for the services they need.

In the Traditional Paradigm, the technical aspects of religious life—prayers, rules, and rituals—defined an organized environment to which religious and clients were forced to adapt. What a symbiotic mode of organization does is make us cognizant of the fact that these are socio-technical systems to which individuals bring their unique contributions and shape its destiny via a process of mutual adaptation (Herbst, 1974). In this process, the technical forms of the life are changed by religious who determine the most effective organizational structures whereby missions and spiritual life can be realized. At the same time, the social life within the organization is altered to recognize individual contributions so they can be channeled in support of mission, goals, objectives, and spirituality.

Again, an example shows how the social and the technical can live in symbiosis in the transformal religious community. In the city where I live, a group of religious men live in community. Each has a special technical expertise related to one of the human services. Their social interaction makes it possible for them to share approaches across fields and to jointly address issues that face clients who are in need of many services. They are so energized by their community life that they have become a force that shapes the human services in our city, a result that would be impossible were they to live and work under the Traditional Paradigm.

Symbiosis also applies to our relationships with our clients. In the Traditional Paradigm, we offered a "one size fits all" service, and clients were forced to take it or leave it. The result was that many clients turned elsewhere or simply gave up in their search for help. In contrast, the Transformal Paradigm recognizes that the client too is in symbiotic relationship with ourselves and our organizations. Today's clients see themselves as unique individuals, with special strengths and weaknesses, who come to us for guidance in the use of the former to overcome the latter. Consequently, we cannot "sell them a standard product." On the contrary, we must negotiate with each client to define a mutually satisfactory relationship that will make the best use of the energy each brings to the service bargaining table.

In these ways, symbiosis defines new opportunities for the religious organization and points to sources of energy that can be tapped to seize opportunity. We can draw upon the insight and skills of both religious and clients to create whole new service patterns that have the power to address emerging human problems. We can create a mode of organization that is able to withstand the tide of change and go forth into a turbulent environment with confidence.

Symbiosis and the Learning Organization

At another level of analysis, symbiosis directs our attention to the capacity of the organization, as a whole, to adapt to its environment. As Peter Drucker pointed out a decade ago, these are turbulent times when organization survival depends upon adaptability, when "Managers have to manage separately the productivity of all four key resources: capital, crucial physical resources, time and knowledge . . . it is the steady increase in the productivities of all resources in their specific institution to which managers must commit themselves in turbulent times" (1980, p.28). This challenge cannot be met unless the organization can learn from its exchanges with its environment, for true productivity follows on the capacity of the organization to increase the energy exchanges with its environment and to deliver value in return for resources and social support.

In his seminal work, *The Fifth Discipline,* Peter Senge takes the position that the learning organization draws on several "component technologies" to adapt to new challenges and opportunities (1991). These have to do with (1) a systems perspective on the organization; (2) spiritual energy; (3) paradigm openness; (4) shared vision; and (5) team learning. When these technologies are present, the organization can indeed learn from its environment and become the vital, adaptive organism existing in symbiosis with its surroundings. Let me offer several observations on these technologies in support of this conclusion.

Systems Perspective: When we knocked down the traditional walls around our organizations, we did so in recognition of the fact that they are *open systems.* This means that they are in active exchange with their environments. The lack of this perspective has made it impossible for religious leaders to anticipate the problems raised by a turbulent environment. For too many centuries, religious communities have been *closed systems,* sufficient unto themselves and oblivious to political, social, and economic forces around them. They have experienced the entropy characteristic of closed systems. By failing to import energy from their environments, they have simply run out of fuel; i.e. religious leaving their congregations and fewer vocations entering them.

In contrast, the open system has the capacity to fight entropy. It can, by the use of what is called *requisite variety,* halt the decay characteristic of closed systems. Requisite variety means that a viable, open system must be at least as complex internally as the environment in which it exists. We can clearly see this at work in our parish schools where whole new functions must be taken on in order to speak to the variety of needs and demands of students and parents. In a sense, religious communities must change from a single, internally-defined service to a supermarket in which options are defined by clients.

Another principle of open systems is that of *equifinality*. This means that many ways exist to achieve the same ends. There is no right way to pursue a given ministry; each of several approaches may be equally valid and/or effective. Equifinality sums up the difference between open—transformal—organizations and their traditional counterparts. Transformal organizations are constantly changing and adapting to their environments. They are energized by their openness to change.

Spiritual Energy: The energizing forces that drive the open system are, of course, the conventional flows of talent, clients, and money. Our organizations could not exist without them, and many of us have become adept at drawing on our environments for them. Although they are necessary, they are not sufficient for symbiosis. In addition, our transformal organization must be vitalized by the spiritual energy of its members.

This idea is easy for religious to accept. After all, isn't spiritual energy what the religious life is all about? The answer to this questions is "Yes, but." The "but" lifts spirituality from a narrow, ritualistic definition to one that looks to the spirit of each religious, every stakeholder, and all clients. Let me borrow from Senge here. (I have replaced his "personal mastery" concept with *spiritual energy*.)

> . . . [Spiritual energy] is the discipline of continually clarifying and deepening our personal vision, of focusing our energies, of developing patience, and of seeing reality objectively. As such, it is an essential cornerstone of the learning organization . . . (for) the organization's commitment to and capacity for learning can be no greater than that of its members. (1991, p. 7)

Spirit gives each of us the energy to learn and the commitment to see the learning process through to a productive end. When our organizations have been transformed in spirit, they have effectively made a new contract with all interested parties. They have agreed to nurture creativity and to seek answers to the most puzzling of human questions.

Paradigm Openness: I realize that the way I have developed the case for the Transformal Paradigm gives the impression that it is the only alternative to the traditional religious life. While I believe it is a viable option to our current modes of thought and organization, I recognize that it is only one of countless paradigms that might give productive form to our futures. There is no ultimate dialectic of paradigms with one clear winner. There are many potential winners, and our vocations call us to a paradigm openness that can give them fair, critical evaluation.

An excellent example of paradigm openness is that of the nursing profession, in which the medical paradigm has given way to a number of alternatives more human and holistic in nature. Practicing nurses are increasingly aware of the fact that high-technology medicine fails to speak to the human needs of their patients. So these care-givers have turned to a holistic view of their clients and opened themselves and their profession to new paradigms—points of view that would have been dismissed as non-scientific (if not heretical) only a decade ago.

Paradigm openness implies that we are able to recognize the ideological roots of our thinking. In practice, it means we reject ideological explanations of reality, and we open ourselves to debate and innovation. Openness is at the core of learning—for we can do nothing new without a readiness to question the old.

Shared Vision: For religious, the concept of shared vision is easy to understand. It refers to a collective understanding of and commitment to the ministry of the organization. Shared vision embraces the mundane activities associated with delivery of human services as well as the lofty goals of dissemination of the Good News. In the transformal organization, shared vision is not some dry, dusty document; it is a vibrant force that motivates every aspect of work and thought.

Shared vision is the working mythology of the organization. For religious, it is a simplified version of the charism of a founder that has real, immediate meaning in everyday life. When Saint John Baptist de La Salle envisioned an apostolate to educate the children of the poor, he surely did not see the modern school in all its technical complexity. Instead, he saw a need that could capture the shared vision of religious across generations. It is only when the De La Salle Brothers lose sight of the vision that they experience frustration. The vision remains clear and adaptable; it is the educational organizations that have become clouded and rigid. They cannot learn because they are no longer populated with individuals who share the vision.

Team Learning: When an organization is populated by those who have paradigm openness and shared vision, it is able to learn. Whether it will do so depends upon the capacity of its members to come together to evaluate alternative paradigms and to shape the vision to the threats and opportunities of the environment.

Not the least of the impediments to team learning is our tendency to let the politics of organization rule the learning process. Too often, we weigh alternatives on the scales of narrow self-interest and value outcomes in equations of power. Team learning is not one of these zero-sum games. It is an integrative process where all parties are guaranteed winners—if they come to the table with openness and vision.

Learning from Mistakes: The above "technologies" do not, it seems to me, tell us all we need to know about the learning organization. We also must recognize that a good deal of learning has to do with taking chances and making mistakes (Argyris and Schon, 1978). This is an aspect of learning that is especially important for religious organizations, where mistakes tend to become permanent ways of life and work.

Learning from mistakes is very likely one of the most significant features of the Transformal Paradigm. It captures the essence of transformation, whereby experience is used to shape the future. The transformed religious life is one in which new ideas and experiments flourish, where every component of the ministry is continually evaluated, and all stakeholders call for an accounting of the benefits derived from the use of scarce human and material resources.

For the most part, learning is a positive dynamic, employing all the "technologies" enumerated above. It is also critical and evaluative, questioning the performance of the organization and searching for new opportunity. These learning experiences do not, however, just happen. They must be managed if they are to occur at all, to say nothing of reaping potential benefit. Organizations learn only when managed, and symbiosis can only be achieved by a learning organization.

Managing Symbiosis

Another way to state the message of this chapter is to note that the complex dynamics inherent in modern society are not absent from church organizations. We can observe them at work in three interlocking sets of forces that define the parameters of organized religious life today. These forces can be thought of as aspects of the environment which, when taken together, tell us what we must do, what opportunities we face, and where our reach is limited. They can be loosely grouped within political, moral-cultural, and economic categories. These three categories are inextricably joined to one another in a symbiotic relationship wherein each contributes to and derives strength from the others. In order to fulfill itself as the holy and mysterious proclaimer of the Kingdom of God and simultaneously serve the people of God seeking that Kingdom, the church and its related organizations need to reckon with this triad of social forces.

The title of these paragraphs, *Managing Symbiosis,* raises the question, "What do managers do when they manage symbiosis?" The answer is that they recognize the influence of the political, the moral-cultural, and the economic aspects of environment on the church and its works. The key word is *management* (DeThomasis, 1984, p. 79 ff).

When we consider the complex needs of individuals and the concomitant stress placed on society and its institutions to satisfy them, it is no wonder that some of us may fall back on the belief that "God will provide." To address the spiritual, physical, psychological, and interpersonal needs of humanity, institutions must be permeated by the organizational power of sound management. The Good News of the Gospel, which brings life to the people of God, must be managed if it is to enrich the lives of those it touches. When the Good News is channeled through the complex organizations of the church, it does not become reality by accident; it must be managed. As Pope Paul VI says:

> It is to all Christians that we address an insistent call to action. . . .
> It is not enough to recall principles, state intentions, point to crying
> injustices and utter prophetic denunciations; these words will lack
> real weight unless they are accompanied for each individual by a
> livelier awareness of personal responsibility and by effective action.
> (*Octogesima Adveniens,* 1971)

Good intentions and good will do not replace management in a world ruled by political, moral-cultural, and economic forces. The church and its related organizations must be managed, precisely because God has created so rich and diverse a human community—the people of God—whose differences are overcome only by achieving unity through trust ,and acceptance in the unifying faith of the Creator. The church and its institutions must "be both Christian enough and pragmatic enough to realize that the pure and simple mandate of Christ to love one another demands that a pure and simple response of our hearts must be joined with the complex response from our minds" (DeThomasis, 1981, p. 41).

Instead of issuing a plethora of directives, ultimatums, decrees, exhortations, and homilies on community, the church must adopt a trusting and supportive management structure so that religious may become enablers of community for the people of God. (Borders, 1982). God is operative in the experience of all peoples. Men and women, lay and religious, each in a unique way experience God's unfolding revelation (Moran, 1970). This great diversity of experience is a potentially rich resource for church organizations. God's revelation is never confined to the experience of a single person or group. This is precisely why management of religious institutions is so important. Management is the only means whereby the dominance of a single view can be avoided. Management is the only way that religious organizations can achieve a fruitful, symbiotic relationship with the political, moral-cultural, and economic facts of today.

MODE OF ORGANIZATION: THE TRANSFORMED RELIGIOUS ORGANIZATION IS A LEARNING SOCIAL SYSTEM THAT DRAWS THE ENERGY TO DO ITS WORK FROM SYMBIOTIC EXCHANGES WITH PEOPLE AND ORGANIZATIONS IN ITS ENVIRONMENT.

References

Argyris, C., and Schon, D. (1978) *Organizational Learning*. Reading, MA: Addison-Wesley Publications.

Borders, W. (1982) "What Makes the Church a Community?" *Origins*, 12(14).

DeThomasis, L. (1981) "Justice Education for the Wealthy," *Momentum*, December.

DeThomasis, L. (1984) *My Father's Business: Creating a New Future for the People of God*. Westminster, MD: Christian Classics.

Drucker, P. (1980) *Managing In Turbulent Times*. New York: Harper and Row.

Herbst, P. (1974) *Socio-Technical Design*. London: Tavistock Publications.

Hubbard, H. (1983) "Planning in the Church: The People, the Tasks," *Origins*, 12(45).

Moran, G. (1970) *The Present Revelation*. New York: Herder and Herder.

Morgan, G. (1986) *Images of Organization*. Newbury Park, CA: Sage Publications.

Paul VI. (1971) "Octogesima Adveniens," Apostolic Letter, May 14.

Senge, P. (1991) *The Fifth Discipline*. New York: Doubleday.

CHAPTER 7

In Pursuit of Social Justice

DIMENSION		TRADITIONAL	TRANSFORMAL
PERFORMANCE		Rituals	Social Justice

The Equation of Performance

In thinking about transformation of religious life, it's important to make a clear distinction between purpose and performance. *Purpose* is about what we do, while *performance* is concerned with how well we are doing it. Thus, the question "What is performance?" is essentially an inquiry into the measurement of our work. It is the force that motivates a search for the indicators that tell us to what extent we are meeting the goals set down in our statements of purpose.

Performance, however, is more than a simple report of the condition of our ministry. It embraces not only the benefits of our work but also deals with the associated costs. I could write the equation of performance as:

$$\text{PERFORMANCE} = \text{BENEFITS} - \text{COSTS}$$

What this says is that performance is the difference between the benefits of our mission and the costs of maintaining our lives and work. Despite the mathematical appearance of this statement, it is almost entirely qualitative in its application. Because we are involved in wide-ranging symbiotic relationships with our clients and the environment, it is necessary to view benefits and costs in very general terms. Let's look at an example to see how performance might be assessed.

Think of a traditional parish school. The benefits of that school flow to the children and families of parishioners who obtain quality education and spiritual guidance. These benefits are supplied by sharing the costs of the school and its staff among all members of the parish. So long as parishioners feel that benefits exceed costs, they will perceive that the school is performing well. Now, suppose that costs increase. Salaries go up, the proportion of lay teachers increases, and parishioners are asked to volunteer their time. At the same time, let's assume that benefits are more difficult to attain: children have greater needs, learning objectives are more complex, and children are distracted by interests outside the school. It's quite easy to imagine that the costs of our school might exceed the benefits it delivers—and that the decline in performance might put the school at risk of closure.

In this example, it's important not to focus on the dollars and cents of performance. Although money is at the center of the problems of many parish schools, it is the qualitative aspect of the equation that defines success or failure of the educational ministry. Put another way, if the children of the parish do *well enough,* and the social and economic costs of the school aren't *too high,* the performance will be seen as *adequate.* Each of the terms in italic represents a qualitative judgment as to where the impressions of benefits and costs outweigh narrow financial considerations.

Put another way, the equation of performance is a statement about the social impact of religious organizations. It speaks about the social consequences of our ministry and the costs that our stakeholders assume. The equation is written in very broad, qualitative language so that it can include all aspects of our relationship with the social ecology in which we live and work.

Social Patterns and Traditional Rituals

The idea of assessing performance as *net social impact* helps us to understand why our traditional apostolates and their associated rituals no longer work very well. In the past, our performance equation was in balance; we delivered benefits in excess of cost, and our apostolates were important contributors to the welfare of our clients. We were integrated into a stable pattern of social life, a useful component of society performing important, if not critical, functions.

The stability of the pattern in which we used to exist was such that our apostolates became fully defined in the rituals of our schools, hospitals, and communities. By training new members for the religious life in these rituals, and by drawing our clients into their observance, we solidified a pattern of behavior that proved to work very well over the centuries.

But social change has broken that pattern forever. Religious, no longer secure in the rituals of the past, are immersed in social turbulence and are accountable for their performance according to a modern analysis of the benefits and costs of their work. Thomas Merton identified the implications of this paradigm shift as early as 1964 when he said:

The monastic community is deeply implicated, for better or for worse, in the economic, political and social structures of the contemporary world. To forget or to ignore this does not absolve the monk from responsibility for participation in events in which his very silence and "not knowing" may constitute a form of complicity. The mere fact of "ignoring" what goes on can become a political decision. (1964, p. 7)

In this paragraph, Merton is redefining the domains of the variables in our performance equation. He is telling us that the pattern has been enlarged from a narrow religious focus to one that is at once economic, political, and social. He has positioned religious men and women in a social matrix where their performance will be measured by the extent to which they contribute to the quality of life of all people.

This is the identical charge given to religious by Pope John Paul II's *Encyclical on Social Concern* in which he states:

I wish to appeal with simplicity and humility to everyone, to all men and women without exception. I wish to ask them to be convinced of the seriousness and to implement—by the way they live as individuals and as families, by the use of their resources, by their civic activity, by contributing to economic and political decisions and by personal commitment to national and international undertakings—the measures inspired by solidarity and love of preference for the poor.

In this commitment, the sons and daughters of the Church must serve as examples and guides, for they are called upon, in conformity with the programme announced by Jesus himself, to "preach good news to the poor . . . to proclaim release to the captives and recovering of sight to the blind, to set at liberty those who are oppressed, to proclaim the acceptable year of the Lord" (Luke 4:18–19). (1987, p. 96)

These challenges represent a paradigm shift in the ways religious men and women assess their performance. They are challenged to see the world through the lenses of economics, politics, and sociology, and to view the consequences of modern development objectively. But more importantly, they are not just observers. When Pope John Paul II quoted the message of Jesus, he was not advocating a preaching ministry. He seemed to be urging on us a course of action that can only be followed outside the traditional patterns of the religious life.

Forging a New Pattern of Performance

If a religious community accepts the new paradigm that requires, without exception, a reintroduction of their founder's charism in terms of effective action for social justice responsive to today's world, then they are ready to take the next steps. But all too often, it is at this point that religious communities turn immediately to injustice in the world around them without looking first to the popularly perceived injustice within the church. How can we hope to change the whole world if many perceive our own house not to be in order?

Surely we cannot expect to be credible advocates for social justice if a growing number of critics, correctly or incorrectly, picture our Holy Father as the most political of pontiffs in recent history. Yet he refuses to permit clergy and religious to participate in the political offices that can give authentic assistance to the oppressed. How do religious communities continue to utilize the vocabulary of a vow of poverty in a world that abhors the thought of poverty and tries to eradicate it? How does the church react to those who hold that while the church advocates the rights of women on one hand, it prohibits their ordination on the other?

We, as religious, must not be afraid to confront these sorts of questions if they are asked in a spirit void of divisiveness, and if they are received without defensiveness by those addressed. In other words, if Christian love is present, then and only then have we taken the first step toward social justice in our own house. Once we have started to question perceived injustice constructively in the patterns of our own lives, we can set out to make specific changes in our ministries in pursuit of social justice. In the following paragraphs, I point to several specific areas in which religious men and women can begin to lay the foundations for social justice.

It would seem that the first area of attention must be the initial formation programs that bring new candidates into our communities. A new approach needs to be taken to these young men and women. They should be prepared to engage in an active religious community committed to social justice in all aspects of its ministry. A community with a rich apostolic tradition must avoid imposing a life of monastic contemplation on a person who is preparing to be socially active. Although candidates are often removed from the material world during formation, it is possible to make that world a part of their everyday lives. Indeed, it is necessary to do so if social justice is to be more than an empty sermon. The notion that a candidate acquires spirituality through monastic contemplation and then takes this new force into the world simply doesn't work. It is bad spirituality and still worse psychology. We should prepare our young religious by integrating spirituality with social action.

The novices who leave the cloistered world of formation are sentenced to great internal turmoil, disenchantment with religious life, and greatly reduced effectiveness when they move into the outside world. What must be understood is that the contemplative life is not better than—it is only different from—the spiritual life of the religious who are actively praying and working to make their prayers a reality. Prayer for the active religious is not a practice, it is an attitude. If we are to measure our performance in the coin of social justice, we need to throw out the monastic rituals of prayer in favor of an active prayer life with the performance of social justice. Prayer is an attitude that necessarily leads to social action, and holiness is being in the world, not above the world.

To move from ritual to social justice requires training for worldly roles as well as spiritual understanding. Economics, politics, and cultural anthropology should be as much part of formation as meditation, prayer, and theology. Not only should these secular topics be studied, they should be practiced. Novices should be involved in corporations, social service agencies, and community action groups to further their understanding of the forces that shape opportunity.

Our first challenge to ritual is to create formation programs that will help integrate the candidate spiritually and actively in the real world that God has called them to serve. Consider Elizabeth Malets's commentary on Thomas Merton's *Transforming Journey.*

> Clearly, Merton had made a "political decision" not to ignore what was transpiring in the world outside the monastery. And that was simultaneously a religious decision for he interpreted his speaking out "not only as a monk but also as a responsible citizen of a very powerful nation" as "a solemn obligation to conscience." By the mid–1980's, Merton saw the social and political positions he assumed as not only rooted in the Gospel but also directly related to his particular commitments as a monk. . . . "To have a vow of poverty seems to me illusory," Merton declared, "if I do not in some way identify myself with the cause of people who are denied their right and forced, for the most part, to live in abject misery." At this

point in Merton's life to identify with the cause of the dispossessed did not mean simply to empathize; it signified that he had to take a stand, put himself on the line, and speak out on the issues with the formidable verbal powers at his disposal. (1980, p. 77)

A second area where the new performance paradigm must take root is in the way the community pursues its ministry. For example, if a religious community has a tradition of operating schools, social justice does not require that they cease doing so. Instead, they should consider the way Sister Jean and her colleagues transformed their traditional school into an organization serving the needs of a new, poor, and increasingly oppressed middle-class clientele. Whatever religious orders are about, they must continually ask the question, "How does our work affect the balance of justice in the social order where we live, and in the larger world?" Let's take the example of an educational ministry a little further.

To operate a "good" school that has "effective" discipline and provides an "academic" education is likely to perform poorly in terms of social justice. To treat the human condition in the abstract is to miss the true meaning of justice. Instead, the "good" school is one that is steeped in the social, political, and moral-cultural climate of our times. Whatever the level of the "good" school, it must graduate students marked with an astuteness that makes them both adept and comfortable in acting as instruments of change to make social justice a reality. This can only be accomplished by educating young people to be participants and leaders in those economic and political institutions where poverty and oppression can be truly alleviated.

But it is not only our clients who must actively pursue social justice. This is a third area in which a new paradigm of the religious life is needed. Some of us need to be trained as effective infiltrators into economic and political organizations. For it is by our direct involvement in these organizations that religious can be the vanguard for positive actions that promote the cause of social justice. This is a real paradigm-breaking act! Isn't it our tradition to not be involved in worldly activity?

Yes, but it is that very tradition that is making us ineffective today. Effective performance is a matter of voting the stocks we have purchased with our pensions and endowments, taking executive positions, and, in some instances, starting our own corporations so that we can use the power of democratic capitalism to the benefit of all stakeholders. Inserting ourselves into the world of business and politics isn't for the sole purpose of acquiring resources to do our religious work better. It is to influence directly that world by becoming powerful in the structures of society. We must not be idle witnesses to our values—we must seek the levers of command to make those values a reality. By our involvement, we can give new meaning to the concept of corporate responsibility, both within and outside organizations.

It is in our influence and leadership that the *greatest* potential for social justice can be found. We can become, in effect, a corporate conscience speaking out for moral principles and ethical behavior. When we do this, we embrace an important trend in contemporary business. Simply stated, ethics in business is good business, and those organizations that can measure their work on the combined scales of profit and social justice will succeed. But they won't do nearly as well if religious men and women fail to take up the challenge of economic and political involvement. We can make these seemingly impersonal organizations into instruments of social justice. Consider how Goodpasture and Mathews make the case for corporate responsibility.

> Concepts like moral responsibility not only make sense when applied to organizations but also provide touchstones for designing more effective models than we now have for guiding corporate policy. We take this position because we think an analogy holds between the individual and the corporation. If we analyze the concept of moral responsibility as it applies to persons, we find that projecting it to corporations as agents in society is possible. (1982, p. 136)

When we become *involved* in the corporations *agency,* we can direct some of its activities to special social justice concerns that may be hidden from other managers. In this way, religious can help shape the corporate conscience and thereby multiply their effect on social conditions.

A fourth area in which the paradigm can be changed is noted above—but it requires separate attention. This is the area of political activity. It is unrealistic to think that social justice can be attained by social and economic institutions alone. Those in need will find only our safety net under them unless we help them to access the political process that has pushed them outside the system.

As in the business world, religious can be most effective by working from positions within the political system. This means that the holding of government and political offices should be considered as one of the instruments of social justice. But this will require the church to examine its prohibitions against political activity.

In considering these options, it is important to note that the real gains in social justice are to be found in the integration of economic and political activities. As we are seeing in Latin America, "A convergence of views between the bishops and the economists . . . [recognizes] . . . that solidarity should be developed within the context of a free, competitive and flexible economy. In other words, a strong market economy would be needed to produce the resources for the state to provide for the poor's social needs. Operationally, this would mean a less interventionist and regulatory state, creating instead the policy environment for economic success, while channeling budgetary resources to assist the poor" (Truitt, 1991, p. A 11). What better agenda for our involvement!

A fifth, more traditional area that we must not forget is that of missions. The familiar scripture from Saint Matthew says it all, "Go forth therefore and make all nations my disciples" (28:19). The implications for religious communities are clear. If we are truly committed to social justice, we cannot be concerned solely with our isolated, national problems. No matter what our transformed mission might be, we are neighbors with millions of people in need. As Father Olowin points out:

> In the teaching of Jesus Christ the 'neighbor' is no longer limited to kin or kind but it is an open-ended title for any human being . . . the world of the New Testament was not an abstraction. The Word made Flesh came to talk to concrete human beings, not human nature or created matter. Jesus Christ was sent to establish an encounter with each individual person. . . . The Gospels are not merely to be tended, they are to be lived and shared with every culture, among every people (1982, p. 2).

It is true that not all religious communities can effectively send personnel to foreign missions, nor are all religious equipped with the necessary expertise to be effective instruments of social justice in other cultures. However, this does not diminish responsibility. We have the capability to direct resources in support of missions and to bring them into concert with working social and political models. This is especially important in those countries where the church has turned to Marxism as a means for social justice. The failed model of communism now needs to be replaced with democratic capitalism, but only where religious men and women are willing to take an active role in shaping its power to the ends of social justice.

Social Justice and Religious Vows

Social justice becomes very personal for all of us as we pursue its ends within the framework of our vows. We need to study the implications of vows and to weigh them on the scales of social justice. Vows must support, not impede, our work in the outside world, and they must define an environment in which each religious experiences social justice in their own life.

Much has been written during the last decade about the social injustices imposed upon religious men and women by the practice of the vow of chastity. Volumes of psychological research have documented the feelings of isolation, loneliness, lovelessness, guilt, and the inability to have close relationships as experienced by religious men and women. The director of the California House of Affirmation wrote, "We find that many of the neuroses we treat are aggravated by styles of spirituality and community life that encourage religious to be slavishly dependent, to intellectualize and mask the so-called negative feelings, and to try to be happy without giving and receiving genuine affection and warm love" (Mehegan, 1982, p. 13). The message here is that social justice for religious is found in improved human relationships and a more holistic understanding and respect for the vow of chastity.

In the same light, serious consideration must be given to the vow of poverty. We must consider that the vow of poverty was originally intended to divorce religious from material things. It was never intended to glorify poverty as a lifestyle. Moreover, we cannot use the benefits of wealth for ourselves and at the same time announce our poverty. Instead, we must see resources as held in trust to be used to further the cause of social justice.

It is also important for religious to explore the vow of obedience. If religious men and women become more actively involved in economic and political life, they cannot be held to narrow definitions of the vow of obedience. In its place, we need to realize that "the final norm of religious life is the following of Christ as it is put before us in the Gospel; this is to be taken by all institutes as the supreme rule" *(Perfectae Caritatis).*

PERFORMANCE: THE PERFORMANCE OF THE TRANSFORMED RELIGIOUS LIFE IS MEASURED BY THE EXTENT TO WHICH THE INVOLVEMENT OF RELIGIOUS MEN AND WOMEN INCREASES SOCIAL JUSTICE FOR ALL PEOPLE.

References

DeThomasis, L. (1982) *Social Justice: A Christian Pragmatic Response in Today's World*. Winona, MN: Saint Mary's College Publications.

Goodpasture, K., and Mathews, J. (1982) "Can A Corporation Have A Conscience," *Harvard Business Review,* January, 132–141.

John Paul II. (1987) *Sollicitudo Rei Socialis*. Washington, DC: United States Catholic Conference.

Malets, E., CSC. (1980) *The Solitary Explorer.* San Francisco, CA: Harper and Row.

Mehegan, D. (1982) "Counseling The Clergy," *The Boston Globe Magazine,* August 15, p. 13.

Merton, T. (1964) *Seeds of Destruction*. New York: Macmillan.

Olowin, Fr. J. (1982) "How Does CODEL, Through Development Activities, Manifest the Unity of the Holy Spirit?" *CODEL News,* May/June, 2.

Truitt, N. (1991) "Latin Bishops Look for Liberation in a Market Economy," *Wall Street Journal*. Friday, May 10, p. A 11.

Vatican Council II. (1965) "Perfectae Caritatis," Decree on the Sensitive Renewal of Religious Life, October.

CHAPTER 8

The Transformal Leader

DIMENSION	TRADITIONAL	TRANSFORMAL
DIRECTION	Administration	Leadership

The success or failure of the transformations discussed up to this point will ultimately depend upon the direction of our religious organizations. If we remain locked in the patterns of bureaucratic administration that have directed our activities in the past, we will be unable to realize the benefits of a transformed religious life. On the other hand, if we are able to identify and foster creative leadership in our organizations, we will unleash the creative power of our congregations to pursue new ministries.

In order to make this transformation, we must attend to two critical aspects of direction. First, we need to replace bureaucratic organizational forms by new, more complex, less tidy structures that can release individual initiative. Then, we must throw over the narrow structural concerns of administration in favor of challenges for effective action posed by leadership. I recognize that these are difficult tasks. In some ways, they are even more challenging than the other transformations about which we have been talking. To move from administration to leadership strikes at the organizational core of the religious life. Where order and routine rule, we must turn to fluid structures that can be re-formed to respond to emerging economic, political, and social developments. Where obedience and conformity are the norm, we must foster critical analysis and self-direction. Single, unified purpose must give way to multiple perspectives and approaches to the ministries of tomorrow.

This is a tall order! Here we are striking at the very structures that have enabled the church to endure the centuries. We are asking the church and our orders to become a part of the world and to work in concert with the people of God. In doing so, we are opening our organizations to social justice. Remember:

> Integral to our mission is our work in behalf of justice and the transformation of the world. Our commitment is to respect the dignity of the human person as the image of God. Our responsibility is to

assure that all systems or structures of an economic, political, social or cultural nature are oriented to the growth and development of the human person. In this way the gospel command of love is instilled into the complex relationship of society. As church, this respect for and commitment to the life and dignity of the human person are at the heart of our faith. (Minnesota Bishops, 1981)

The charge posed by this view of purpose is to make the people of God an integral part of our organizations. As we do so, we must be prepared to give leadership to our joint work so that we can multiply the effect of our energy and resources. Let's see how this might be done.

Transforming the Religious Organization

The organizational model I am proposing here is based on an interactive process for church management, a process rooted in the spirit of Vatican Council II. It is an attempt to present an image that will lead to a dynamic that fully recognizes the dignity and freedom of all the people of God within an organized church and in conformity with the teachings of the magisterium concerning ecclesiology. To realize this goal, both people and church must change: the first to be loving and responsible participants, and the second to guide the faithful in our responsibility to enhance the church of Jesus Christ in the modern world. Make no mistake, this is a difficult task, and both the people and the church must give freely to the common cause.

The organizational changes we are talking about here must be substantive, not merely symbolic. It's not enough to create a machinery for participation. That participation must be real; it must be respectful of the magisterium who are the stewards of the true Gospel message; and it must be led, not managed. Hear Father Murnion, then director of the U.S. Bishops' Parish Project, on this point.

The growth of participatory process in the church while rooted in Vatican II, is also part of a development that occurred in all of society in the late '60's. Almost every institution, challenged by its constituents about the extent to which it was serving the needs of the constituents, developed some form of constituent participation. Thus we have community-planning board, hospital boards, school boards, university senates and the like. All appear to be suffering the same lack of clarity about their relationship to the executive officers of their respective institutions, a condition exacerbated by both the simultaneous growth of the bureaucracies in these institutions and the very multiplication of such councils. (1981, p. 153)

Father Murnion further explains that at the parish level, this same confusion is experienced in unclear relationships among priests, parishioners, pastors, councils and staff. This experience infiltrates most of the church and its related organizations. The fostered image is that of a lack of consistency in the church. While we hear much about shared responsibility, many complain that what they actually experience is an "owner" religious or clergy utilizing lay people primarily as fund-raising instruments. At the level of the diocese, the typical sharing is between priests and bishop, and in religious orders, between the congregation and its superiors. On the level of the universal church, the image of dialogue is restricted to pope, Curia, and bishops. There is no image of shared responsibility between leaders and the people of God.

If this flawed image is to be transformed, we must devise organizations that bring people and leadership together. As I see it, this can be accomplished by putting leaders at the focal point of the interaction between the people of God and the organizations of the church. To help you visualize how this might be done, I will use two triangles similar to those presented in Chapter 5. However, this time they will meet at their points rather than at their baselines.

In this way, I wish to illustrate the twofold, yet integrated structure needed to accomplish the purpose of a church organization. This structure (not to be confused with an "ecclesiology") includes (1) the purpose itself, and (2) the realization of that purpose. Each of these aspects of organization has its own distinctive process and dynamic whereby it integrates people and structure. As we can see in Figure 8.1, these two participants are brought into focus by a Chief Executive Officer. This is the individual who must lead in the transformed religious organization.

The reader will note that this drawing is somewhat paradoxical. Although I am using it to advocate *leadership* and *reorganization,* it gives the familiar appearance of *hierarchy.* But this is not its intent. The levels in the two triangles above are meant to indicate *functions* that must be performed in the organization. The structure that ultimately results from a sharing of these *functions* will be relatively *flat.* It may well place the religious CEO at the center of a number of level interactions. It is not likely that such a role would be placed at the top of a pyramid of authority. If such a pyramid were to be the results of our transformal efforts, we

FIGURE 8.1

PEOPLE AND ORGANIZATION:
THE LEADERSHIP INTERFACE

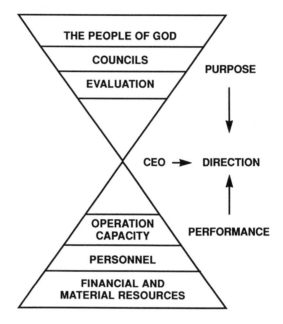

would surely have failed to bring our lives and work into the next millennium.

As I proceed with a discussion of leadership, the reader should keep all of the italicized words in the above paragraph in mind. They are the concepts that a transformed religious organization should incorporate in its new design. No drawing or diagram is adequate to this task; we can only use these pictures as a visual aid for our imagination. Bearing this in mind, let's see if we can make Figure 8.1 work for us.

One way to soften the hierarchical view of the above structure is to see the CEO *at the bottom* of the top triangle. All communication originating from the people of God filters through committees and councils to the CEO. That person does not dictate to the people. Instead, the CEO receives the people's vision of purpose and attempts to effect it through those who populate the bottom triangle. Thus, the CEO is a responsible communicator who gives leadership through both vision and the manner in which she or he organizes and motivates the congregation.

The Evolution of Purpose: Purpose does not spring, ready made, from the people. It must be carefully developed and structured so that each stakeholder has personal input and is confident that purpose is reflective of individual needs and desires. This truly turns the daily functioning institutional church (not an "ecclesiology") on its head. Purpose arises from the dialogue and prayer of the people, not from a vision handed down by administrators.

In other words, Figure 8.1 is an attempt to effect the ordinary organizational functioning of the church and congregations. It is a possible schematic representation of Vatican Council II and Pope John Paul II's view of co-responsibility and participatory involvement of all the faithful in the church (Origins, 1978). The people's vision of purpose—the modern ministry—begins with their life experiences in a process of self-actualization. With prayer, dialogue, and discernment of the Spirit, and through their human experience of community, the people of God create a genuine locus of God's unfolding revelation.

However, human difficulties arise when the people attempt to articulate God's revelation into meanings that can guide their actions. Here is where leadership is absolutely necessary in order to create opportunities for dialogue and insight. Leaders become resources from which the people can draw to inform their debates and shape the process of consensus building. In so doing, leaders bring all the resources of the religious organization to the table to assist the people.

At this point, we need to consider how purpose becomes ministry and how ministry is translated into specific objectives within the religious organization. Notice that these objectives are not created in the upper triangle of Figure 8.1, they are *evaluated* by agents of the people. The people—the stakeholders—create a vision of purpose that expresses their beliefs and aspirations. These are combined and refined into specific ministries that describe in very general terms how the activities of religious organizations will be directed at purpose. For example, the people might be concerned over the plight of the homeless among them. In their debates, the people might decide that their religious activities ought to center on serving the homeless. That purpose could then become a ministry to the homeless that would focus the attention of religious men and women on this particular set of stakeholders. The ministry to the homeless becomes a reality when leadership succeeds in translating it into specific objectives with associated measures of performance.

In Figure 8.2, I try to show the steps through which the concerns and visions of the people of God become objectives that guide our own work.

FIGURE 8.2

LEADERSHIP AND THE EVOLUTION OF SOCIAL JUSTICE

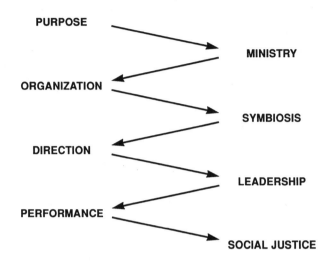

Notice how the key dimensions of our paradigm shift appear in this process. Purpose becomes ministry through the control of stakeholders. By using a symbiotic mode of organization, the people link themselves to their environment. Through the direction of leaders, the religious organization ensures that its performance on its objectives will meet the test of social justice. Thus, the Transformal Paradigm is an integrated response to the ecclesial challenge of Vatican Council II, a way to make church and people one.

Another way to look at Figure 8.2 is to see it as the process whereby a relatively subjective purpose becomes concrete performance. Examined from this perspective, we can visualize the flow of belief into action; we can measure the extent to which our performance makes our beliefs a reality. This is precisely where the traditional religious organization comes under question. Its performance is no longer representative of the foundational beliefs of its stakeholders. It cannot draw on the energy and commitment of the people because its purpose is at variance with their basic needs and aspirations. This is exactly what the modern religious leader must attend to; the leader must articulate the vision of stakeholders with the performance of colleagues.

The leader responds to this challenge by working within the functional areas pictured in the lower triangle of Figure 8.1. Responding to information concerning financial and material resources, personnel knowledge and skill, and operational capacities, the leader must shape performance objectives that are expressions of purpose, yet attainable within the capacity of the organization. This process takes place at the interface of our two triangles. The CEO, the leader, puts performance objectives in a form that representatives of the people can evaluate. Leaders chosen by the people interact with the CEO and other religious leaders in the process that matches performance to purpose.

Once there is agreement on performance objectives, it is the responsibility of leaders in the bottom triangle to initiate and manage activities whereby these objectives are realized. These leaders are accountable for integrating all aspects of performance and assessing the extent to which objectives have been met.

This sort of response is in sharp contrast to the traditional religious organization. In most of these structures, there is no way to hold administrators responsible for performance. It is this lack of accountability that results in many people viewing the church and congregational stewardship of material and human resources in a poor light (DeThomasis, 1989). By making ourselves accountable, by measuring our performance, we forge a new relationship with our stakeholders, one that promotes the self-actualization of all people of God.

The Self-Actualizing Structure

Can an organization be self-actualizing? Can the impersonal structures that guide our daily work help each of us be self-actualizing? Can the totality of the religious organization help the people self-actualize? I believe that the answers to these questions is a qualified "yes." It is qualified in that we must bring structure and process together so that our activities and their consequences address all of the psychological components of self actualization.

I have seen these self-actualizing consequences in some aspects of many religious organization. However, none has the broad-gauged capacity to self-actualize that is required by the Transformal Paradigm. The reason for isolated instances of self-actualizing religious organizations lies, I firmly believe, in the leadership of our congregations. In the past, we have elected administrators rather than leaders. Those who directed our orders and organizations were too much concerned with bureaucracy and too tightly linked to the machinations of hierarchical structures. This resulted in a stifling environment where self-actualization was difficult.

The leadership of the 1990s will need to overcome the administrative practices of the past in order to give undivided attention to self-actualizing processes. The focus of these new leaders must be bi-directional; they must attend to networking with the people of God while, at the same time, executing the purpose arising from the people. These are leadership functions that run in parallel with the purpose-performance continuum. They are another side to the organizational vision discussed above.

FIGURE 8.3

THE SELF-ACTUALIZING ORGANIZATION

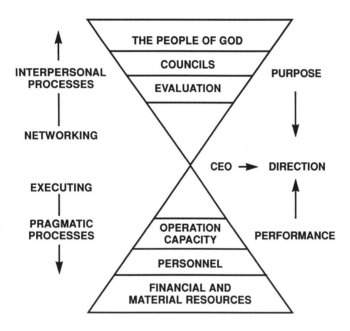

What I am trying to say in Figure 8.3 is simply this: If the church or any of its related organizations are to express concretely the love to which Jesus Christ called them, then those organizations must be motivated by the faith-filled spirit of individuals as the church actually becomes church through the liberating dynamics and the process of a self-actualizing organizational structure. In this process, leadership involves guiding the people of God to articulate their many purposes with the knowledge, skills, and commitment of religious.

Although leadership must be widely diffused throughout the structure in Figure 8.3, how it comes about is necessarily focused on the chief executive officer. For the way the CEO plays the executive role will define leadership for all others in the structure. This is due to the fact that the CEO manages two quite distinct spheres within the organization. In this model, leadership strives for respect for the process of self-actualization of its members as individuals while embracing the communal dimensions of organizational life. These two spheres, which I call networking and executing, call for different methods of leadership.

In the *networking* mode, the CEO is at the bottom of the set of forces emanating from the people of God. This is a role that is supportive of the process of God's continued revelation through the interpersonal lives of the people. The leader is intimately involved with this process in order to develop the self-actualization of the people as church through their vision of purpose. In effect, the CEO is called upon to give leadership to the people of God as they develop purpose. As a leader, the CEO must be intimately present to all the people, not as a boss but as a facilitator, dreamer, animator, and motivator. Leadership in this sense involves those qualities that facilitate the people in open dialogue.

The choice of the term *networking* captures the essence of leadership as a dynamic that assists the people of God in their search for self-actualizing purpose. First of all, it involves an inversion of a hierarchical structure. We must turn that hierarchy on its head, exactly as it is shown in the above drawings, to put the people of God at the focus. In this inverted hierarchy, leaders shape purpose by networking and by arranging where the people talk to each other, and where they share ideas, information and resources. Leaders who are effective networkers can create opportunities for communication, facilitate interactions, and mediate disagreements. They are the collegial, the participators, the questioners, those who are centered on the identification and evolution of purpose. Their charge is to create networks that serve the dignity and freedom of the people to help them see themselves as liberated Christians, self-actualized people who manifest God in their purpose and actions.

Now consider the process of executing as it is pictured in the bottom triangle of Figure 8.3. Here the CEO is at the top of pyramid. Doesn't this contradict the entire argument of self-actualization? It does only if the triangle stands alone. When it is coupled with the upper triangle, the position of the CEO is quite different. It signifies that the CEO is empowered through self-actualization of the people of God. The CEO has helped the people identify the purposes of the church and has become their voice, speaking to the religious community with the authority of the people.

In the organizational role, the CEO draws on the various "capacities" (operations, personnel and resources) to transform purpose into performance so that it can be *executed*. In this use of the word, I mean to convey the sense of execute as leadership. Each of the capacities must have its own executive if the structure is to be truly self-actualizing. Another way to say this is that the CEO must be free to *lead* and must, therefore, be supported by other religious who can assume executive roles within each capacity.

For example, the traditional parish school is customarily administered by a principal who is personally responsible for all its activities. The principal must not only pay attention to the overall performance of the school but must also direct instructional operations, recruit and manage personnel, and keep a close watch on all aspects of resources. With this collection of responsibilities, the principal is not free to lead. In fact, the principal is barely able to juggle a set of complex demands. The result is that nobody is satisfied. The people who are concerned with the school are alienated from its activities. Teachers feel that they have no real voice in determining how the purpose of the school is to be realized. And students become regimented in operations that often have little relevance to their everyday experiences outside the school. This is a structure that cries out for leadership and for self-actualization of the organization and all its members and stakeholders.

Leaders have cut through this tangle to make their schools self-actualizing organizations. The key to this success is the shift of authority and responsibility to those most closely involved with students. Each counselor and teacher, each secretary and janitor, has a stake in the purpose of the school. Since they have ownership, they take their responsibility seriously. They can take actions and make decisions to meet the immediate needs of their clients. Surely, they are wrong at times, but they learn from their mistakes, a small price to pay for a school that is responsive to the risks facing its students.

In organizations, the self-actualization potential is without limit. All members of the staff can reach as high as they wish and can make the best use of their God-given talents. In the resulting learning environment, both teachers and students can rise above their immediate circumstances. This definition captures the essence of *leadership:* the creation of opportunity for all involved in the organization.

Practicing Leadership

The challenge I've set for the transformal leader may seem to be impossible. There probably aren't enough exceptional individuals to lead all our religious organizations. This means that leadership must be shared among us and that each religious person must assume a personal share of the leadership functions. Thus the choice of assistants, committee chairs, and other key personnel is a critical aspect of leadership. All leaders must pay close attention to the needs of the organization and to the strengths and weaknesses of those who might respond to them. This includes the leader as well. Knowledge and skill must also be analyzed objectively, with compensation and support provided where someone falls short.

To make use of the self-actualizing model, it's helpful to take a drawing like Figure 8.3 and "fill in the blanks." Each of the six levels in the model should be filled with notes that describe the organization and how it will interface with its stakeholders, the people of God. In the upper triangle, this requires identification of leaders among the people and assignment of purpose-related responsibilities. It also involves provision for coordination of their work so that it "adds up" to a view of purpose that can be met by organizational performance.

On the lower triangle, each aspect of the organization —operations, personnel and resources—must be articulated with performance. This too requires identification of leaders whose talents can make these *capacities* come together so that they speak to the purpose as it is seen by the people of God. As these "blanks" are filled in, the self-actualizing organization becomes reality. I would, however, offer one cautionary note. Leaders must take care to make participation and dialogue a means, not an end in itself. The organization must continually take care not to become paralyzed by processes of consultation and consensus building. It must always be led, lest it become a forum for opinion. Remember, the self-actualizing organization is going somewhere. It is not static, it is purposeful. And it is measured by the extent to which its performance results in true self-actualization of those in and around it.

DIRECTION: TRANSFORMED RELIGIOUS COMMUNITIES ARE LED BY INDIVIDUALS WHO UTILIZE INTERPERSONAL AND PRAGMATIC PROCESSES TO ASSIST ALL INVOLVED IN MOVING TOWARD SELF-ACTUALIZATION.

References

DeThomasis, L. (1984) *My Father's Business: Creating A New Future for the People of God.* Westminister, MD: Christian Classics.

DeThomasis, L. (1989) *Monasteries on Wall Street? The Commandments of Doing Ethics In Business.* Winona, MN: Saint Mary's College Publications.

Minnesota Bishops. (1981) "Employers and Employees in the Church," *Origins,* 11(1), 9.

Murnion, P. (1981) "The Unmet Challenges of Vatican II," *Origins,* 11(10), 150–155.

Origins. (1978) 8(19), 291–294.

CHAPTER 9

From Providence to Potential

DIMENSION		TRADITIONAL	TRANSFORMAL
RESOURCES		Divine Providence	Human Potential

When I made the case for shifting our resource base from Divine Providence to human potential in Chapter 3, I was hoping to draw your attention to the fact that the religious community must depend upon itself rather than waiting for God to come to its rescue. In the context of the self-actualizing organization, this means that each of us must understand our human potential and continually seek ways to add our contributions to the performance of our organizations. To do so, we must take both a "hard" and a "soft" perspective on ourselves; we must be at once hard, quantitative managers of our resources and works as well as soft, qualitative human beings who assist one another in the process of self-actualization.

If we view this challenge from a traditional perspective, we conclude, at best, that we need a division of labor in our organizations with some of us serving as managers, others as counselors. At worst, we might decide that the "hard" and the "soft" cannot be addressed within religious organizations. Two examples will show that these traditional perspectives are ineffective in the modern world.

First, let's think about the "division of labor" approach. This is the way most dioceses are organized. The bishop takes care of the souls of the congregation and speaks, as best he can, to their need for self-actualization. Business managers, either lay or religious, watch over the physical and fiscal resources of the diocese. And never the twain shall meet! This perspective leads to two worlds that are forever separate. Neither can draw upon the potential inherent in the other. As a result both are weakened, and the diocese cannot respond to the social ecology around it.

Second, consider the religious congregation that decides to forego involvement with material things to do the work of the Spirit. This is typified by a group of sisters who recently sold their hospitals in order to use the proceeds to work with the homeless. Already they are at the mercy of consultants charging large fees to show them how to manage the proceeds of their sale. It will be but a few more years before the proceeds have disappeared, and only a few homeless will have been served. In this instance, the desire to be free from materialism has destroyed the capacity to serve those in need. It would have been far better to continue operating the hospitals, using their profit to provide an ongoing ministry to the homeless.

In these two simple, real life examples, we can see the need to consider how our human potential is supported and enhanced by our physical and financial resources. This is not a schizophrenic view of religious organizations. It is a necessary condition for dynamic self-actualizing organizations that can take their strength from active participation in their economic, political and moral-cultural environments.

The Material Foundations of Human Potential

While the transformed religious organization is founded on deep spiritual commitment to social justice, it is energized by people who use the material foundations of their organizations in new ministries. I firmly believe that the Holy Spirit is the all-powerful force that guarantees our performance. However, if we fail to manage our material resources, we will be severely limited in our ability to reach out to the growing numbers of needy people. In other words, we need to pay close attention to the factors that determine our performance capacity.

Performance capacity can be thought of as resting upon three "pools" of resources (Ammentorp and Grass, 1981). These are shown schematically in Figure 9.1.

Each of these "pools" contributes its potential to performance capacity in a more or less effective way, depending upon how the resources in the "pool" are managed and how they are brought to bear on performance in a coordinated way.

Maximizing Material Resource Potential: For too long, religious communities have held themselves at arm's length from their material resources. They have squirreled away the cash donations of parishioners, left enormous sums in non-interest bearing bank accounts, and lost precious dollars through imprudent investments and purchases. Fortunately this lack of good stewardship of resources is diminishing, but it is still prevalent in many ways.

Our past failure does not mean that we must continue down the path of imprudence. Instead, we must realize that the material resources at our disposal are provided for us in trust for the people of God. We must exer-

FIGURE 9.1

**UNLOCKING HUMAN POTENTIAL
IN RELIGIOUS ORGANIZATIONS**

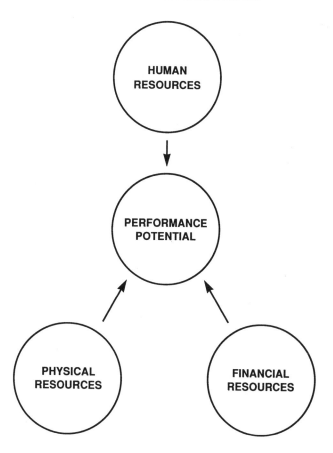

cise our stewardship over these resources so that their potential can be fully utilized. This is a two-part responsibility related to stewardship and fiscal management.

Stewardship of material resources is a relatively new concept for religious organizations. Heretofore we have assumed that our status as religious communities implied that any resources entrusted to us would be in the care of reliable stewards. This is an assumption that does not hold up under test. Many, if not most, religious organizations do not understand the nature of stewardship, nor do they know how to go about exercising it.

The essence of *stewardship* is that those who give resources to an order or organization can be secure in the knowledge that every dollar will be put to use in ways that are consistent with the ministry of the organization. Stewardship goes beyond the purposeful use of resources; it is combined with fiscal management and includes *prudence* in the management of funds, *control* over their expenditure, and *accountability* for the results achieved through their use. The steward is, in effect, expected to act much as the "good and faithful servant" who was able to multiply resources in the parable of the talents.

Prudent fund management means that the value of resources not yet expended will be preserved. Investments must, at a minimum, compensate for inflation, and they must track economic growth rates so that their potential impact is enhanced over time. Prudence also implies protection such that inordinate risks are avoided, and investments are legally secure whenever possible. These aspects of prudence cannot be left to "experts" outside our organizations; they must be responsibilities taken on by our own leaders. If this means that many of us must be trained in the arcane arts of financial investment, so be it.

Control over material resources is a matter of careful preparation and management of budgets. Religious can no longer expect to dip into petty cash and bank accounts at will. Instead, each of us must coordinate our work and our needs for support through the mechanisms of the budgetary process. The purposes of our ministries must be translated into dollars and cents so that it is clear how material resources are applied. Once a budget has been adopted, it must be managed so that expenditures are controlled according to standard accounting practices.

Although we must follow the principles of accounting, we must also be accountable. Those who supply our material resources must be able to find out how effective we were in using their contributions to achieve our purpose. To answer their questions, we must be able to link resources to performance. As an extension of our answers, we must identify both successes and failures and be ready to respond to the concerns of stakeholders.

I cannot leave the area of stewardship and fiscal management without sharing an experience I had recently that sums up the need for these leadership skills. The president of a religious college asked me to visit his campus to assist with a "financial problem." When I arrived on the campus, I met with the controller of the college and asked for the college's bank records. Imagine my surprise when I was told that there had been no reconciliation of those records for several months! As I probed more deeply into the financial affairs of the college, I discovered that many student bills were paid in cash, and no system existed to ensure that the cash was properly recorded and credited to student accounts.

The upshot of my experience at this college was that I saw incredible lapses of stewardship and financial management. Not only were the daily financial affairs of the college controlled in an unprofessional, if not illegal, manner but the college was also guilty of a further violation of stewardship. I discovered that they had been balancing their books by selling some very attractive parcels of land to developers. They were eating their seed corn to fill the current harvest table (DeThomasis, et al., 1991).

The Potential of Physical Resources: The example of unfaithful stewardship told above contains another lesson for us. The college was, in a sense, "place bound." It saw itself as a collection of buildings and physical resources located in a given town, dedicated to a specific purpose. This is all well and good so long as that purpose is viable and can be supported by the religious community and its stakeholders. When the time comes that purpose can no longer be supported by the social ecology, we must be ready to vacate our physical premises to pursue our ministry in other settings. In other words, we must define ourselves in purpose, not in bricks and mortar.

This does not mean that we should be like the sisters who sold their hospitals to serve the homeless. It does mean that we must be analytic in our assessment of the economic costs and benefits of our physical resources. This is a matter of balancing a simple equation:

PHYSICAL RESOURCE VALUE =
PURPOSE CONTRIBUTION − COST

This equation must always be in positive balance. That is, contributions must always exceed cost, where both are measured on a real dollar scale.

When we use such an equation to manage physical resources, we must take care to account for *all* contributions and costs. We do so by measuring the current market value of physical resource contributions: the price of square footage of space, the value of housing, and the rental prices of equipment. Against these numbers, we must consider depreciation, debt service, and operating costs of our physical plant. The point where it is cheaper to purchase our physical needs in the open market than to provide them ourselves, we may be at risk of becoming "place bound."

But suppose that the above equation is in balance or that it is positive, and contributions exceed cost. Then it is our task to exercise stewardship over the resources to keep them in good repair and to seek operational efficiencies. We must also consider the possibility that evolution of our purpose will make our physical resources obsolete, even though they are carefully maintained. The needs of our ministries determine the required potential of physical resources. This too must be continually monitored to make sure that we will be able to respond to the changing needs and priorities of the people of God.

The Potential of Human Resources: The contribution of human resources to the ministry potential of our organizations can be weighed much as we have calculated the potential of physical and financial resources. In fact, it's possible to put a value on the contributions each of us make and to compute a sort of "net worth" of our human resources.

This sort of economic approach may turn you off at first. It takes a rather narrow economic perspective on our work and neglects much of the self-actualizing message. Despite the hard-hearted nature of this point of view, it is the essential basis for any self-actualizing organization. The reason for the importance of an economic analysis of our human resources is that no organization can be self-actualizing unless it is soundly positioned in all spheres of human endeavor: economic, political, and moral-cultural. In our haste to do good works in political and social arenas, we generally neglect the economic facts of life and put our organizations at risk.

To show how this works, let's consider the relationship between a typical Catholic college and its human resources. The typical college has gone through a transition and it has established a fair market price for all faculty members, lay and religious alike. When religious contribute their salaries to the college, these funds are accounted for as gifts, and the college has a good sense of the value of its human resources. This is okay so far as it goes. However, few if any colleges consider the *current market value* of human resources. This is not the salaries paid to faculty members. Instead, this is the sum of what the *market* would pay for the faculty members. These numbers can be quite different in those cases where we overpay faculty members who are out of date in their field, or where we underpay those whose special expertise can command a higher price in the market. And, no college I know of takes the trouble to invest in its faculty in any systematic way in order to compensate for the depreciation of its intellectual resources.

This example teaches two important lessons. First, human resources have a value in the market. Each religious man and woman could command a salary commensurate with the value the market places on individual skills. When these salaries are summed across all religious in an organization, we have a measure of the total current market value of our human resources.

The second lesson is more complex. It is based on the notion that our knowledge and skills are volatile. Unless we continue to invest in them, they will depreciate, and our value in the market place will be diminished.

These two lessons tell us that human resources must be managed just as if they were economic goods. Their value must be calculated and maintained if their true potential is to be realized. The hard part of these lessons has to do with the need to invest in people. For too long, we've thought of investments like education as "favors" to the recipient, and not as maintenance of our human resource base.

Once we have accepted the principle of valuing our human resources, we can manage this asset in concert with physical and financial resources. This is a matter of evaluating the ministry potential of each resource base and looking at the aggregate to determine our capacity to realize our performance objectives.

Taking the Measure of Our Resources: While it's easy to say that an economic approach is needed, some very hard questions must be answered in the process. Here are a few examples:

1. Do our physical resources support our ministry? This is basically the issue of being "place bound" in our work. It's really a two-part question that looks to both the direct and indirect mission support given by physical resources. In the direct sense, we need to determine whether our physical environment is the best place for conducting the activities of our ministry. In the indirect sense, we need to ask whether other groups are better equipped to be the location for our ministry.

2. How can our financial resources be used most effectively? In other words, we need to know the "social return" on our money. For instance, the nuns who sold their hospital to use the money for the homeless might have better effected that ministry by multiplying the resources through continued operation of their hospital. To answer the question, we must cultivate a long-range view of our work and a stewardship attitude toward our financial resources. Only then can we expect to invest them wisely and to build a sound basis for future ministries.

3. How can our human resources be utilized most effectively? This is by far the most difficult question. It asks us to look objectively at the knowledge, skill, and aspirations of each religious and to compare individual contributions with others in the market. Then we must ask whether we are the best qualified for the ministry we have in mind. Or, can someone else do a better job?

As we answer these questions, we must be prepared for some surprises. Our ministry may no longer be possible in our physical surroundings. Our financial resources may do more good for more people if they are not expended directly in the activities of our present efforts. And, it may be that other individuals and groups can carry out our ministry more effectively. These are the "down sides" to an assessment of potential. The "up sides" are equally possible. The physical resources we have may be unique, and they might present special environments that can evoke feelings and activities that can be found nowhere else in society. Our money may be the "tipping factor" that releases a wave of concern and action, and its impact might well be multiplied by non-market forces. We too may be the most well-qualified for our ministry, and there may be no better use for our human resources.

In the language of the economist, we are creating an *objective function* that assesses the contribution of each resource pool to the attainment of the goals of our ministry (Keating and Keating, 1980). By recognizing that this function is made up of three components, we have given our leaders a powerful set of levers that can be adjusted to make our organizations more effective. These levers can also be used to create an environment in which self-actualization is possible, for religious men and women, for the people of God, and for the organization itself.

Self-Actualization of Human Potential

Self-actualization must, of course, go well beyond the narrow economic analysis discussed above. It involves our deepest personal feelings on one hand, and the social environment where we live and work on the other hand. By taking a truly humanistic perspective on these two aspects of self-actualization, we can unlock the tremendous potential held by ourselves and our organizations.

Let me return to Maslow to give our discussion a focus on what is meant by self-actualization of the individual. He saw the self-actualizing person as one in whom,

. . . the conative, the cognitive, the affective and the motor are less separated from each other and are more synergic, i.e., working collaboratively without conflict to the same ends. The conclusions of rational, careful thinking are apt to come to the same conclusions as those of the blind appetites. What such a person wants and enjoys is apt to be just what is for him. (1968, p. 208)

For the modern religious, to be self-actualized means that one's deepest spiritual feelings are given visible form in professional life and the activities of daily living. Everything "hangs together" for this person. To be self-actualized, in this sense, is very likely what many of our founders had in mind when they set out to create communities of people who would live out their vision of spirituality.

When we look back on the rather chaotic pattern of religious life in the last two and one-half decades, we see religious men and women striking out in search of self-actualization. Many turned to the professions to attempt to integrate their values and work, only to be frustrated by narrowness of purpose and emptiness of value. Others retreated to the cloister in the hope that ritual and routine would liberate the self, only to have these hopes dashed by the irrelevance of their lives. Still others turned to prayer and contemplation in the belief that spiritual energy would fulfill their innermost personal needs, only to discover that the spirit requires action to give it healing power. In all these attempts, religious were looking to the *components* of self-actualization without recognizing that all aspects of self must be drawn together to liberate human potential.

In my call for the transformed religious life, I am challenging every religious to examine all facets of the self. The Transformal Paradigm presented throughout this text is like a set of tools the individual can use to break down the barriers that have compartmentalized religious life in the past. Once these barriers, and those in our own minds, are leveled, we can look to the unique power each of has to carry the message of Christ to the people of God.

To be self-actualized is to be an individual: a person whose vision of the ministry is unique, whose activities give personal expression to the mystery, and whose life is an example that truly glorifies God. In Joshua's words:

Each apostle must be free to work with his own flock, and solve the unique problems of his own flock, with the different cultures and languages and understandings of life. The Spirit must be able to move freely and exercise His freedom in different ways and in different forms, and freely express Himself through a variety of gifts and not through sterile uniformity, which merely satisfies man's need for security. (Girzone, 1987, p. 263)

Girzone's *Joshua* challenges us to be individuals, to actualize ourselves, and to celebrate our uniqueness. He recognizes that the people of God come in many forms and that cultural differences may define self-actualization in a variety of special ways. This is another example of the symbiotic link between religious and the people of God. As we find our own identities in service, we become a part of the process of self-actualization of the people.

The release of human potential through self-actualization is one that vitalizes our work and our organizations, but only if the organization itself actively promotes and supports the individual's search for meaning.

From this point of view, a society or a culture [or an organization] can be either growth-fostering, or growth-inhibiting. The sources of growth and humanness are essentially within the human person and are not created or invented by society, which can only help or hinder the development of humanness, just as a gardener can help or hinder the growth of a rosebush, but cannot determine that it shall be an oak tree. (Maslow, 1968, p. 211)

Here is the essence of the Transformal Paradigm shift of resources from Divine Providence to human potential. It is a turning away from the notion of a religious community as a definer of the identities of its members in favor of organizations that offer options and help each person develop individual human potential. Insofar as we are able to transform our organizations in this direction, we will harvest the fruits of the tremendous human potential in our congregations.

RESOURCES: THE TRANSFORMAL RELIGIOUS ORGANIZATION IS VITALIZED BY CREATIVE USE OF HUMAN POTENTIAL IN THE APPLICATION OF PHYSICAL AND FINANCIAL RESOURCES TO THE ATTAINMENT OF GOD'S PURPOSE.

References

Ammentorp, W. and Grass, P. (1981) *Financial Management of Not for Profit Institutions*. Winona, MN: Saint Mary's College Publications.

DeThomasis, L. (1978) *The Finance of Education*. Winona, MN: Saint Mary's College Publications.

DeThomasis, L., et al. (1991) *The Transformal Organization*. Winona, MN: The Metanoia Group.

Girzone, J. (1987) *Joshua: A Parable for Today*. New York: Macmillan.

Keating, B., and Keating, M. (1980) *Not For Profit*. Glen Ridge, NJ: Thomas Horton and Daughters.

Maslow, A. (1968) *Toward A Psychology of Being*. New York: Van Nostrand.

Miller, J. (1978) *Living Systems*. New York: McGraw-Hill.

CHAPTER 10

Transformation and Imagination

DIMENSION	TRADITIONAL	TRANSFORMAL
DYNAMIC	The Rule	Imagination

Paradigms cannot be separated from their driving force(s), the dynamic that energizes people to put the paradigm to work in their organizations (DeThomasis, et al., 1991). Without their associated dynamics, paradigms are merely intellectual exercises in organizational analysis. Thus, the Rule gave traditional religious a reason for every action and an overall concept of how their work related to the larger purpose of the church. Surely each of us can recall how our vows gave us the psychic energy to devote our lives to the purpose of our order.

The same can be said for the Transformal Paradigm. It too must have a dynamic that can interest men and women in its new dimensions and excite them to a transformed purpose. This dynamic is *imagination,* the ability to visualize new paradigms and their implications for individuals and organizations. It is a dynamic of special significance for religious leaders, those who must break the Traditional Paradigm. And the evidence is clear. Those who have used imagination in the past have been successful in adapting religious organizations to new realities. They are like the business men and women Anthony has in mind when he writes:

> Down through history, the determining factor between leaders who were effective and those who were not has been the acuity of perception. Those who chose to utilize their imagination and creativity have gone forward, while those who relied on their power and dominance have not. (1988, p. 105)

This observation is especially important for religious leaders, as it draws a clear contrast between those who have relied on bureaucratic authority and those who elected to imagine alternative organizational forms and purposes. It is an observation that asks us to explore how imagination can be applied to each of the dimensions we have been discussing.

In the paragraphs below, I will reiterate the essential messages of the Transformal Paradigm. These principles pose the major challenges we face as religious communities, and they set out the first steps we must take in transforming our lives and work. As you review them, bear in mind that I am talking about *transformation,* not merely *change.* As Sammon points out, these are not merely different names for the same thing.

> Change and transformation are not the same. For example, change happens at a point in time; transformation happens over time. Change is a new beginning; transformation begins with an ending. While change can require people to make a transformation, the latter allows for the spiritual and psychological reorientations that need to happen for people to find meaning in any changed situation. (1991, p. 190)

The key point in this view of transformation is that the organization or institution that is being transformed must end before it can begin anew. Thus, the religious life as we know it, the Traditional Paradigm, must give way to a totally new view of every organization dimension. In order for these new views to emerge, each of us must give free rein to our imagination and call up new ways of thinking, being, and serving from the foundations of our commitment to the religious life.

Imagining Transformed Purpose

> PURPOSE: RELIGIOUS MEN AND WOMEN ARE ENGAGED IN THE MINISTRY OF ACTION. THEY ARE ACTIVELY INVOLVED IN MAKING ECONOMIC, POLITICAL, AND MORAL DECISIONS BY WHICH THEY DEFINE THE MESSAGE OF CHRIST IN THE HUMAN CONSEQUENCES OF WHAT THEY DO.

The central theme in Transformal Purpose is that of *action.* Although we may be divided in how we approach purpose, we are at one in our commitment to action. With this shared commitment, community life can become a forum for discussion of alternative actions in which religious men and women can challenge one another in a productive search for those strategies that "work."

Contrast such a transformed community with the soporific environment that traditional purpose has produced. This has been characterized by Arbuckle as a sort of "club," where we sleep our lives away in blissful ignorance of the outside world.

> So community life is shallow and apt to be more to the "boarding house" or "gentlemen's club" style—pleasant, but definitely not threatening, for real issues that might divide are avoided and individual independence is carefully observed. (1988, p. 83)

How easy it is to let one's imagination sleep in an environment where the old paradigm is firmly entrenched in the politics of community life. In fact, if we do not put an end to traditional forms and rituals of religious life, we will fail to explore the new paradigms that may revitalize our commitment.

An examination of purpose is the way we break with the past and build the connections for new bridges into the future. Religious leaders, and by this I mean all religious who have a vision of the future, must imagine transformed purpose as well as the actions that will realize the associated goals. Although I have emphasized action in my earlier discussion of purpose, I want to be absolutely clear that there must be a fundamental human aspect to the way we imagine our future work.

To *be* a religious person, particularly someone truly human, is greater Christian witness than being able to *do* something. Accordingly, the purpose of all religious orders must always emphasize our commitment to all people and to the liberation of their lives and spirit. This applies both to the immediate purpose of life in community as well as to the larger purpose achieved by religious men and women. We must first look inward and examine current rituals, practices, and ministries to see whether they humanize the religious life. Then, when our houses are in order, we must look outward and shape our purpose so that we truly transform social, economic, and political realities to the benefit of all people. When we have created an environment in which such comprehensive reviews of purpose are possible, we will be able to imagine communities and ministries that have the capacity to transform.

Imagining Transformed Control

CONTROL: ALL STAKEHOLDERS ARE INVOLVED IN DE-FINING THE ORGANIZING PARADIGM FOR A LIVING CHURCH—ONE THAT ENERGIZES PEOPLE TO PURSUE

SELF-ACTUALIZATION AND PROVIDES A SAFETY NET FOR
THOSE WHO FALTER IN THEIR QUEST.

What this principle does is recognize that imagination is not a gift given only to a few selected religious leaders. It is a resource that is broadly diffused among all the people of God. It only needs to be called out by religious organizations to become a force that can truly transform our joint futures. This is a true metanoic, or transformal, experience for most religious; a shift of mind from an authoritarian church to a *living church*.

The living church of the future is also a self-actualizing church. It provides the spiritual framework within which each person of God can find higher states of being and acting. This is a framework lighted by imagination; each person imagines how the self can both fulfill the mundane requirements of daily life and lift up the soul to a confirmation of self in God. Imagination is what makes the church alive—an environment in which all people explore how they might more productively use their own gifts in relationship to one another.

It is in the exploration of imagination in the living church that religious men and women have so much to contribute to the people of God. We can liberate the imagination of each person to help that individual envision a future where aspirations can be realized. In so doing, we are instruments of social development; helping each person utilize God-given abilities and helping them shape social and economic realities to their own needs.

There is, however, another side to self-actualization. That side involves putting the *self* in second place to *other,* an acknowledgment of our shared humanity. To make sure this aspect of self-actualization occurs, religious must act as a "social conscience" to question those who are self-centered and who pursue their own ends to the detriment of others. We can help these persons imagine how the pursuit of social justice, in cooperation with other people of God, can enhance the self-actualization of everyone.

As we imagine control, we need to keep these two ideas in mind. First, there is a need to open the church to stakeholders so that each person can enter into the debate over what the living church is to become. Second, a balance must be struck between self-centered pursuit of personal goals and self-actualization as it is made possible through joint pursuit of social justice. As these ideas develop in the years ahead, I am confident that we will see the church truly come alive with the imaginative contributions of all of the people of God.

Imagining Transformed Religious Organizations

MODE OF ORGANIZATION: THE TRANSFORMED RELI-
GIOUS ORGANIZATION IS A LEARNING SOCIAL SYSTEM
THAT DRAWS THE ENERGY TO DO ITS WORK FROM SYM-
BIOTIC EXCHANGES WITH PEOPLE AND ORGANIZATIONS
IN ITS ENVIRONMENT.

The two words we need to keep in mind concerning the mode of organization are *learning* and *symbiotic*. They set the stage for imagining forms
of organization that represent true alternatives to our Traditional Paradigm. Make no mistake, there *will* be new paradigms. Their myths,
metaphors, and models will be determined by our imagination and the
shape of our organizations will be defined by how we imagine our work
and life.

In times of paradigm shifts, the only surviving organizations will be
those that are able to *learn*. Experimentation, evaluation, success, and
even failure become the defining characteristics of life in the learning organization (Senge, 1991). They characterize both the organization as a
whole and the experience of the individual, for organizations cannot learn
unless each member is also an active learner. Each of us must become
what Donald Schon has called the "reflective practitioner," a person
whose life is a continual cycle of imagining new goals and ways of attaining them, and evaluating the results so that the cycle can be repeated
(Schon, 1983). As more and more religious become "reflective practitioners" and put their imaginations to work, our organizations will lose
their rigidity and begin to learn new ways of relating to their surroundings and to the people of God.

The learning organization does not exist in isolation from the social
ecology around it. As the organization becomes dedicated to learning, it
opens its boundaries to the environment and experiences increased exchanges with other organizations and individuals. These exchanges are
the occasions for learning and for moving the organization into a symbiotic relationship with its environment. Symbiosis can take two very different meanings. It can imply a passive response to the stimuli of the
environment where the organization learns what to do and what not to do.
On the other hand, symbiosis can mean that the organization is not only
learning but is an active force that *causes* learning in its environment.

Imagination makes it possible for both organization and environment
to learn through symbiosis. The Transformal Organization not only learns

about itself and its potential, it is a teacher of other organizations and people. Imagination helps us reach out to others and assist them in transforming their social, economic and political futures. This is true symbiosis—mutual evolution toward a collective self-actualization.

Imagining Transformal Performance

PERFORMANCE: THE PERFORMANCE OF THE TRANSFORMED RELIGIOUS LIFE IS MEASURED BY THE EXTENT TO WHICH THE INVOLVEMENT OF RELIGIOUS MEN AND WOMEN INCREASES SOCIAL JUSTICE FOR ALL PEOPLE.

As I pointed out in Chapter 7, performance and purpose are two related views of the way we define our apostolates and missions. Purpose states what we are about, and performance is a measure of how well we do it. In general, performance has a very practical orientation that centers our attention on the costs and benefits of our work. But as the above principle shows, this is not a cold-blooded calculation of the dollars and cents of religious work. The assessment of performance is, in the transformal religious organization, an expansion of purpose—a way to make sure that our actions "add up" to the achievement of social justice for all people.

When we think of performance in this larger sense, it is clear that imagination has a critical role to play in the measurement of our work. Imagination causes us to look to less tangible evidence when we assess purpose. We are no longer limited to counting the numbers of clients we serve, nor to measuring the improvement in their health and well-being. Instead, our attention is directed to the ways our lives, works, and institutions work together to improve the lot of all the people of God.

Here is the essence of imagination at work. By viewing performance in these broad terms, we are able to turn away from ritualistic calculations of limited apostolates. Imagination encourages us to re-define the charisma of our founders, to transform that vision into missions and services of relevance to modern society. In a very real sense, imagined performance encourages a re-founding of our orders, breathing new life into visions that time may have rendered irrelevant (Cada, 1979).

Imagining a transformed purpose requires a shift of focus from individual clients to larger groups of people. Where once we were able to count our accomplishments in terms of the number of students we graduated or the number of patients treated, we must now think of changing organizations or whole political systems. The reason for this is twofold. Our numbers are such that we no longer have the multiplying effects of the past. These must be replaced by the work of fewer religious to make broader social changes. Imagination is a critical ingredient in shifting our focus, for we must break with traditional measures of performance and replace them with indicators that are sensitive to the gradual impact of our work in ever-larger social systems.

This does not mean that we must neglect those individuals who want and need us. What it does mean is that we must use their experiences to question and change institutions in imaginative ways. When one of our minority students complains about harassment, we must deal with the case in a personal and supportive way. But we must go farther than that. Through that person's experience, we must see a need for attacking the attitudes and actions that foster hate in our society. Imagination helps us see the need for social action in the everyday problems of the people of God and adds new, broader dimensions to our performance.

Imagining Transformed Direction

DIRECTION: TRANSFORMED RELIGIOUS COMMUNITIES ARE LED BY INDIVIDUALS WHO UTILIZE INTERPERSONAL AND PRAGMATIC PROCESSES TO ASSIST ALL THOSE INVOLVED IN MOVING TOWARD SELF-ACTUALIZATION.

I have already stated the obvious: religious leaders are the embodiment of imagination. No religious community can hope to transform itself or those it touches without an imaginative leader. It is also clear that leaders are responsible for helping the rest of us apply the Transformal Principles. Given the case for imaginative leadership, which is a strong one, how can leaders articulate their vision with other religious, clients, and key actors in the environment?

I believe that the answer lies in the way leaders define paradigms. More specifically, I see the leader's imagination at work in the myths and metaphors proposed as alternatives to those of outmoded paradigms. For it is through myths and metaphors that leaders give form to their vision of the future and excite others to follow or to challenge new paradigms (Owen, 1987). Let's see how this works by considering the juxtaposition of traditional and transformal myths concerning leadership.

Traditional leadership mythology: In the Traditional Paradigm, leaders are selected for their ability to hold the community to the Rule and to the apostolate defined by the founder. The resulting mythology has the leader speaking *for* or *as* the founder, with complete authority over all religious and clients. The associated metaphor is that of the flock, where the leader is shepherd and all others, sheep. As the flock moves along the path mapped by the founder, the shepherd sees to it that wayward sheep are brought back into the fold and that their basic needs are met by the flock.

Traditional leadership mythology has no place for imagination. Any attempt by a member of the flock to deviate from the predetermined path is deviation, not imagination. Although this stifles change and creativity, it is quite an effective metaphor so long as the environment remains placid and pastoral.

Transformal leadership mythology: Here, the myth changes, and the leader has a vision of the future. The transformal leader is much like the founder in that imagination may create a vision that has the potential to be charismatic. More accurately, the myth pictures the leader as a transformer, one who can overthrow or redefine ruling paradigms.

Where the transformal leadership myth departs from the traditional is in the metaphor. There are as many metaphors at work in the transformal religious organization as there are leaders. And leaders gain credibility and authority as their imagination stands the test of application. When vision "works," it may lead to a metaphor of the life as a corporate entity, or even a metaphor of community as a family farm. The point is that metaphor is not settled in transformal religious organizations. It is the living stuff of imagination, the language whereby religious express their commitment to the organization and its purpose.

Imagining Transformed Resources

RESOURCES: THE TRANSFORMAL RELIGIOUS ORGANIZATION IS VITALIZED BY CREATIVE USE OF HUMAN POTENTIAL IN THE APPLICATION OF PHYSICAL AND FINANCIAL RESOURCES TO THE ATTAINMENT OF GOD'S PURPOSE.

It often seems that people are the problem for many religious orders. Individual religious demand that they define their own mission and all elements of personal lifestyle. Religious communities literally fly apart as they try to accommodate people who often have nothing in common but their avowed Catholicism. As communities have tried to be all things to all religious, they too have drifted away from the charisma of their founders and become blundering searchers for impossible solutions. People are the problem.

In the transformed community, people are the solution. Their many and varied imaginative visions of the future provide the alternatives that a vital community must possess in order to exist in a turbulent ecology. Since their energies are no longer dissipated in struggling with traditional metaphors and models, they are free to test their imaginations in action and to select the futures that fulfill their shared purpose.

Imagination: The Dynamic of Transformation

In this book, I have tried to set out a vision of the future that religious men and women can use as a sounding board against which they might test their own imaginations. The Transformal Paradigm is not a specific plan for action. Rather, it is a vision that may or may not excite others to explore the challenges and opportunities of the future. The paradigm I've outlined, therefore, is not to be taken as new doctrine but as a means to unleash the forces of creativity that reside in all religious.

Kathleen Popko captures the essence of my message when she writes:

> This dream of social transformation will arise not from some centralized, formal plan plotting each step, but from the aggregate of many social forces, many individual attitudinal shifts and collective choices. Quantum physicists addressing social change suggest that change takes place when there are enough pockets of energy in many places to generate a shift in consciousness. (1991, p. 222)

Imagination is that energy, the dynamic that will position the religious life for a productive transition to the new millennium. The imagination dynamic is different from the other Transformal Principles in that it must be stated as a challenge. This is because imagination is not static. It continues to suggest new visions of the religious life that can keep the church alive in whatever ecology may evolve in the years ahead.

DYNAMIC: LET US, INDIVIDUALLY AND TOGETHER, SET OUR IMAGINATIONS FREE TO DISCOVER TRANSFORMED

RELIGIOUS LIVES THAT MEET THE CHALLENGES AND OP-
PORTUNITIES OF THE NEW MILLENNIUM WHILE PRE-
SERVING THE ESSENTIAL CHARISMA OF CHRIST.

References

Agor, W. (1984) *Intuitive Management*. Englewood Cliffs, NJ: Prentice Hall.

Anthony, E., et al. (1988) *Envisionary Management*. New York: Quorum Books.

Arbuckle, G. (1988) *Out of Chaos: Refounding Religious Congregations*. New York: Paulist Press.

Cada, L. (1979) *Shaping the Coming Age of Religious Life*. New York: Seabury Press.

DeThomasis, L., et al. (1991) *The Transformal Organization*. Winona, MN: The Metanoia Group.

Owen, H. (1987) *Spirit, Transformation and Development in Organizations*. New York: Abbott.

Popko, K. (1991) "Contemplating Religious Life's Future," *Origins*, 21(14).

Sammon, S. (1991) "The Transformation of the Religious Life," *Origins*, 21(12).

Schon, D. (1983) *The Reflective Practitioner*. New York: Basic Books.

Senge, P. (1991) *The Fifth Discipline*. New York: Doubleday,

Wittberg, P. (1991) *Creating a Future for Religious Life*. Mahwah, NJ: Paulist Press.

THE TRANSFORMAL PRINCIPLES

PURPOSE: RELIGIOUS MEN AND WOMEN ARE ENGAGED IN THE MINISTRY OF ACTION. THEY ARE ACTIVELY INVOLVED IN MAKING ECONOMIC, POLITICAL, AND MORAL DECISIONS IN WHICH THEY DEFINE THE MESSAGE OF CHRIST BY THE HUMAN CONSEQUENCES OF WHAT THEY DO.

CONTROL: ALL STAKEHOLDERS ARE INVOLVED IN DEFINING THE ORGANIZING PARADIGM FOR A LIVING CHURCH—ONE THAT ENERGIZES PEOPLE TO PURSUE SELF-ACTUALIZATION AND PROVIDES A SAFETY NET FOR THOSE WHO FALTER IN THEIR QUEST.

MODE OF ORGANIZATION: THE TRANSFORMED RELIGIOUS ORGANIZATION IS A LEARNING SOCIAL SYSTEM THAT DRAWS THE ENERGY TO DO ITS WORK FROM SYMBIOTIC EXCHANGES WITH PEOPLE AND ORGANIZATIONS IN ITS ENVIRONMENT.

PERFORMANCE: THE PERFORMANCE OF THE TRANSFORMED RELIGIOUS LIFE IS MEASURED BY THE EXTENT TO WHICH THE INVOLVEMENT OF RELIGIOUS MEN AND WOMEN INCREASES.

DIRECTION: TRANSFORMED RELIGIOUS COMMUNITIES ARE LED BY INDIVIDUALS WHO UTILIZE INTERPERSONAL AND PRAGMATIC PROCESSES THAT ASSIST ALL THOSE INVOLVED IN MOVING TOWARD SELF-ACTUALIZATION.

RESOURCES: THE TRANSFORMAL RELIGIOUS ORGANIZATION IS VITALIZED BY CREATIVE USE OF HUMAN POTENTIAL IN THE APPLICATION OF PHYSICAL AND FINANCIAL RESOURCES TO THE ATTAINMENT OF GOD'S PURPOSE.

DYNAMIC: LET US, INDIVIDUALLY AND TOGETHER, SET OUR IMAGINATIONS FREE TO DISCOVER TRANSFORMED RELIGIOUS LIVES THAT MEET THE CHALLENGES AND OPPORTUNITIES OF THE NEW MILLENNIUM WHILE PRESERVING THE ESSENTIAL CHARISMA OF CHRIST.

ALTERNATIVE* PARADIGMS FOR
THE RELIGIOUS LIFE

ORGANIZATION DIMENSION	ALTERNATIVE PARADIGMS	
	TRADITIONAL	TRANSFORMAL
PURPOSE	Apostolate/Ministry	Transformation
CONTROL	Congregation	Stakeholders
MODE OF ORGANIZATION	Bureaucracy	Symbiotic
PERFORMANCE	Rituals	Social Justice
DIRECTION	Administration	Leadership
RESOURCES	Divine Providence	Human Potential
DYNAMIC	The Rule	Imagination
SOCIAL ECOLOGY FOUNDATION		

* The term *alternative* does not imply that the two paradigms are mutually exclusive, that the Transformal Paradigm should replace the Traditional Paradigm. Thus, Imagination does not replace the Rule as the organization's dynamic; Imagination is a new way of transforming the Rule so that it becomes an effective dynamic for religious communities.